"For many years Gary Burge has focused on issues relating to Palestinians and the land of Israel. In this careful survey of biblical material, he pulls the rug from under any Christian emphasis on a special status for the land of Israel and from under Christian Zionism. Churches and pastors need to give serious attention to this study and follow its lead."

—**Klyne Snodgrass**, North Park
Theological Seminary

"Once in a while a book comes along that reshapes the theological landscape. This is such a book, and it is destined to become a defining text on the biblical theology of the land. Gary Burge carefully and systematically reveals the way in which Jesus and the apostles understood how the Abrahamic covenant to the land would be fulfilled. He shows how in Jesus Christ the promises made to Abraham embrace not only the Jewish people but all peoples and indeed the entire cosmos. *Jesus and the Land* is a magnificent book—a 'must read' and a point of reference for all concerned with a thoroughly biblical theology of the land as well as the causes of the Arab-Israeli conflict."

—**Stephen Sizer**, author of *Zion's Christian Soldiers?*
The Bible, Israel, and the Church

JESUS AND THE LAND

The New Testament Challenge to "Holy Land" Theology

GARY M. BURGE

Baker Academic

a division of Baker Publishing Group
Grand Rapids, Michigan

Published in North America by Baker Academic
a division of Baker Publishing Group
P.O. Box 6287, Grand Rapids, MI 49516-6287
www.bakeracademic.com

Published in Great Britain by Society for Promoting Christian Knowledge
36 Causton Street
London SW1P 4ST

Printed in the United States of America

Library of Congress Cataloging-in-Publication Data is on file at the Library of Congress, Washington, DC.

ISBN 978-0-8010-3898-3

11 12 13 14 15 16 17   8 7 6 5 4 3 2

Contents

Contents

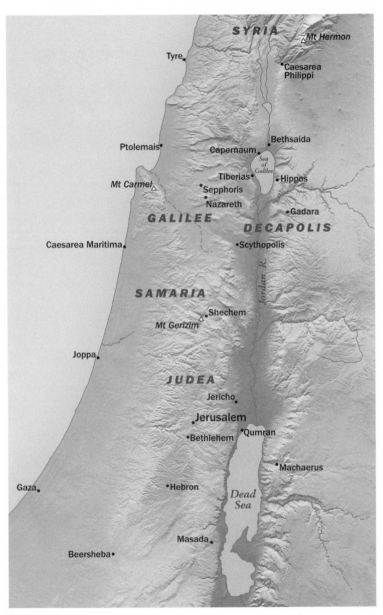

The Holy Land in the first century

Introduction: land, place, and religion

Land is potent not simply because it represents geography we may own, but because it represents a place where we are rooted and can understand who we are. While most cultures around the world understand this notion intuitively, our modern Western world often lives with a sense of displacement, a yearning to find a place where identity may be securely held. When an American tells a visitor from Europe that her ancestors are from France or perhaps Germany, she may be referring to events 150 years ago; the American is holding on to an ancestral identity that has only the remotest connection to her present life.

It is an understandable desire. Each of us wants a place that we can call home, a place we may think of as our own, where familiar things are available, where old stories may be retold, where we experience some connection with a legacy that stretches out behind us. My grandparents saved for years to make the fabled trip "home to Sweden and Germany." And there they hoped to discover their separate roots and recover something of who they were by filling in the stories that they heard as children from their parents. When I first moved to Chicago in the 1990s, my grandparents were delighted. They grew up in Chicago as a part of the Swedish and German immigrant communities. When they visited they were eager for me to take them to Andersonville – the remnants of the Swedish community that thrived from about 1890 to 1940. They were a part of that community for decades. The church where they married still stands, virtually the way it was in 1920. When my grandmother walked down the aisle again nearly 50 years after her wedding, when she saw the murals and the altar in the church unchanged, she felt rooted, anchored in history and time.

Places have a unique power for each of us – and they can inspire us to build great things or they can lead to devastation and suffering. When *place* is tied to *religion*, suddenly the forces that these two represent become doubly potent. Suddenly I can make claim to a place because my God has given it to me.

In 1987 the Serbian leader Slobodan Milosevic rallied support among the Serbs in Kosovo by giving a now-famous speech in the Polje town hall in central Kosovo. It seemed incidental at the time but it propelled Milosevic to power. Then in 1999 during the Kosovo war, it suddenly all made sense. Milosevic was no fool. He spoke to the Serbs evoking ancient memory claiming that this region, this land of Kosovo, belonged to them by divine right. At the time Kosovo was chiefly Muslim but the Christian Serbs held a grudge that was 650 years old. This had been historic Christian land and they had come to retake it.

Here is the background. On June 15, 1389, this site – known as Blackbird Field – is where 25,000 Serbian soldiers met 40,000 Ottoman troops in what would be considered the defining battle of Serbian cultural identity. The Ottoman armies won but the event crystallized Serbian resistance against Islam and continues to live even today as a symbol of land lost and land that must be reclaimed. In 1987, Milosevic was standing on that famed fourteenth-century battlefield when he said to his Christian Serb audience, "No one has the right to beat you…No one will beat you ever." Blackbird Field was as much symbol as it was territory. To possess it helped define Serbian self-determination. He was evoking an amalgam of feelings: historical, cultural, and religious. This is where Muslims killed Christians. And it would not happen again. Over twenty years later, when Kosovo declared its independence on February 17, 2008 (with American backing) it was no surprise that Serbian crowds (with Russian backing) expressed outrage. On February 21 approximately 200,000 Serbs gathered in central Belgrade and by night's end, the US embassy was in flames.

Human history is littered with such stories. Europe is replete with claims and counter-claims for land that has been lost and land that will be reclaimed. Land is not simply about possessing real estate; land is about security and identity, it is about cultural cohesion and purpose. Land in its most profound sense is about place, possessing a locale which is ours, which can be defended, which can give us safety from the world. And frequently, land-claims are linked to religious commitments.

This easily describes the tribal life of ancient Israel. Land boundaries were an important part of Israelite settlement in Canaan. God had granted this land to each tribe as a heritage. And that struggle to hold this land, to protect those settlement boundaries, was acute right through the biblical period. Life in the land of promise was intimately connected to life within God's covenant. To live outside the land of promise seemed inconceivable.

But the same observations can be seen today in the same geographical regions that witnessed struggles between the Israelites and their many neighbors (see map, p. viii). Where the Moabites, Edomites, and Egyptians pressed Israel's borders, today similar land struggles no less vicious are a regular occurrence. Arabs lived in this place called "Palestine" for centuries alongside very small Jewish communities. But then in the early twentieth century a religious vision called Zionism sought to reclaim land that was a part of the old Jewish biblical heritage. Palestine was to become Israel. And in 1948 this vision became reality.

The Israeli–Arab wars of 1948, 1967, 1973, 1982, 2006, and 2009 (joined by two Palestinian uprisings) made clear, however, that these struggles were not simply about the defeat of an opponent. It was about the struggle to possess land, to create a cultural and religious place, to build something ethnic: an exclusively Jewish nation. It is no accident, for instance, that Israel carefully emptied or destroyed over 400 Arab villages in these wars and did not permit their fleeing residents to return.[1] Graffiti written by Israeli soldiers in occupied villages announced that the Arabs would be pushed "into the desert." Few better examples could be found in the twentieth century of a modern nation-state using ancient religious land claims to advance its purposes. But now look at the flip-side. Arab calls could be heard to empty Palestine of Jews, pushing them into the sea. For some, Palestine was Arab land being stolen by Jews. Israel might eradicate an old Arab cultural heritage. Jerusalem is Islam's third most holy city. And Muslims were called out to protect it. In the end, of course, Israel won this struggle and the world's largest refugee crisis resulted. Israel possessed the land, but at a high cost to many.

This religious instinct to attach oneself to land is not regressive or some remnant of ancient religion that needs to be discarded. It is quite normal throughout the world and if anything the modern West is an exception. But there is a double bind that comes with the Holy Land (or the land of Israel). If the Jewish people are the indigenous people of this land, then the Palestinians are indigenous nowhere. And if the Palestinians are indigenous there, then the Jewish people are indigenous nowhere.[2] The more Jews and Palestinians appeal to their exclusive ethnic or religious claim to the Holy Land, the more each will alienate the other.

The resolution of these competing claims for land today will frequently be found in each community's religious framework. Muslim attachment to Jerusalem springs from Muhammad's famous night-time visionary ride on his steed Al-Burak to Mount Zion (Qur'an, sura 17.1). Even the "far mosque" (today in Arabic, the Al Aqsa Mosque) is mentioned. Jews will mention divine promises to Abraham (at this point still called Abram) and his descendants (Genesis 12.1–3; 13.14–17; 15.18–20), realized when the Israelite tribes settled in Canaan.

This book asks how Christians should understand these competing land claims. Given our theological framework, what is the relationship between land and theology in the New Testament? What did Jesus and the New Testament writers think about the territorial claims of ancient Israel? Did they retain the view of the sanctity of Jerusalem and its Temple? Were they rethinking the relationship between faith and locale? Or were they confident that a sacred place was still to be held for believers?

We must admit to a complication within this theme. Land is connected to a network of theological ideas in biblical theology (such as covenant) and when we consider one category, another is inevitably affected. For instance, Jerusalem and its Temple were the focal points of Jewish life in the first century. But if the New Testament reexamines the significance of the Temple and its place, assumptions about territory and religious life will shift as well.

Perhaps for Christians this subject has an application that transcends conflicts in places such as Serbia and Israel. The struggle for land is so deeply imbedded in the human soul – it is so central to our way of viewing the world – and it has led to so many devastating wars, to rethink land and its value might well be another form of the gospel needed desperately in a modern age.

I owe many thanks to those who encouraged this study and urged me to keep at a subject that is as controversial as it is important. The book was originally suggested by Bruce Longenecker, who read the manuscript carefully and provided many helpful comments. James Ernest at Baker Academic did the same and wisely redirected my argument at many points. Rodney Clapp at Baker (USA) and Rebecca

Mulhearn at SPCK (UK) both encouraged the project and brought it to press. The manuscript itself was skillfully edited by David Sanders, who weeded out blunders everyone else missed. The index was produced by my research assistant, Laura Gerlicher, who one day will be writing books of her own. Finally, a note about the cover picture. In June 2009 my wife and I were in Jerusalem staying in the Christian Quarter of the Old City and one day discovered the wonderful photography studio of Mr George Kahvedjian and his son (Elia Photo, 14 Al Khanka Street, <www.eliaphoto.com>). George's father, Mr Elia Kahvedjian (1910–99), was a Jerusalem photographer during the British Mandate period and took numerous pictures of the country before 1948. The Kahvedjian family today sells these magnificent photographs exclusively in their shop. This one shows the city of Jerusalem from the Mount of Olives at sunset in a view now lost to us. Many thanks are due to the Kahvedjian family for the privilege of using a part of their family's legacy in honor of Mr Elia Kahvedjian.

A problem of names

The subject of the Bible and the Holy Land is perhaps one of the most volatile issues of our day. We can find ourselves enmeshed in modern controversies simply by the language we use. In Israel, most admit that *everything* is political, from the restaurants you choose to your home address. Jewish Israelis even have the habit of referring to their neighbors as "Arabs" and not "Palestinians" lest they acknowledge that this is a people with a cultural identity or national aspirations. Scholars have a long tradition of simply referring to the land as *Palestine*, a legacy that began in AD 135 with the Roman emperor Hadrian. Hence scholars frequently refer to Palestinian Judaism to distinguish it from Jewish life outside the Holy Land.

Yet "Palestine" too is filled with political meaning to those Christian and Muslim Arabs who were dispossessed by the Israeli state and yearn for their own place. *Israel* is of course a term with a biblical legacy but it too runs aground in the controversies of modern politics. Is referring to the West Bank as Israel to deny Palestinian plans for those hills? Worse still is the name "Judea and Samaria" for the hills south and north of Jerusalem. This is the preferred title among highly politicized Jewish settlers and Christian and Jewish Zionists. But this is to play to a militant territorial ideology I'd rather avoid.

Names such as "Land of Promise" or "Promised Land" evoke memories of God's covenant gift to Abraham and they might serve us. Christians have a long legacy of referring to this place as the *Holy Land* (Latin, *terra sancta*) and this convention seems a good one. "The land" is also useful since in biblical thought this is land *extraordinaire*. This is Holy Land inasmuch as it became the stage of God's revelation in history. In the first century, the Romans called this province *Judea*. For the period of the New Testament, this is a fully appropriate name and one which I will use. If I wish to refer to the modern state of Israel and the Palestinian territories under occupation (Gaza and the West Bank), I prefer to use the inclusive term, Israel–Palestine. At least this term acknowledges that two peoples live in this place and struggle to understand how they might share its future.

Soli Deo Gloria

1

The biblical heritage

Walter Brueggemann is correct when he suggests that *land* might be the central theme of biblical faith. "Biblical faith is the pursuit of historical belonging that includes a sense of destiny derived from such belonging." And if this is so, he continues, *land* might be a way of "organizing biblical theology."[1] Brueggemann invites us to think carefully about (biblical) Israel's experience with land along three trajectories: *land promised, land possessed, and land lost.* And in each of these categories we can discover the magnificent opportunities found in God's grace and covenant, Israel's historical struggles to possess this land in righteousness – to become the sort of people God intends – and the judgment that falls on Israel in the exile when all is lost. The exile crisis of the sixth century BC is not simply a crisis of land loss, it is the loss of life and hope and meaning when Israel (through its sin) no longer can live in the place of promise.

The interest of the Old Testament however falls on one land, "the land," the "promised land," which is different from every other land. Ezekiel refers to it as the center of the earth (38.12) and Jerusalem as the center of this center (5.5). Hence in all of creation, this land is set apart, for as we shall see, God has unique purposes for it and will describe it as his own.

The Old Testament promise

In Genesis, land is a gift from God from the beginning of creation. The appearance of "dry land" (Gen. 1.9) is set in contrast to the chaotic sea (Ps. 104.5–9). In creation, land can welcome life, land can provide safety and refuge (Jonah 1.9), it represents a place where all people, and in particular the descendants of Abraham, can anchor their culture and nation. In this sense, land is already seen as a gift of creation in Genesis. It is a place God carves out of the world that holds the chaos of the seas at bay.

1

A variety of Hebrew terms represent the ideas of land in its more nuanced uses: there are open fields, orchards, pasture land, desert land, and dry land. A very common noun is *'adama*, which refers to the agricultural qualities of land, as soil or fields (Gen. 2.7; 3.19; Prov. 12.11). But without doubt the most common term is *'ereṣ*, and while a precise distinction may be uncertain, *'ereṣ* often represents land as geographical or political territory. This is the "land of heritage" (Gen. 11.28; Jer. 22.10). It is used for tribal territories as well as the nations who live there (e.g. "the land of Canaan").

The original call of Abraham in Genesis 12.1–3 promises that he will be the father of a great nation, and yet no promise of land is heard until Genesis 13.14–17 when Abraham scans the country he enters for the first time. The formal promise of land is given its full shape in Genesis 15.18–21, "On that day the LORD made a covenant with Abram, saying, 'To your descendants I give this land, from the river of Egypt to the great river, the river Euphrates, the land of the Kenites, the Kenizzites, the Kadmonites, the Hittites, the Perizzites, the Rephaim, the Amorites, the Canaanites, the Girgashites, and the Jebusites.'" The promise is repeated in Genesis 17.7–9 and then it is repeated again for his descendants Isaac (Gen. 26.2–4) and Jacob (Gen. 28.13–15). In each case four themes are clear: (a) Abraham will receive land as an everlasting possession; (b) Abraham's posterity will become a great nation in this place; (c) this promise is directly tied to the covenant; and (d) all of the people of the earth will be blessed by this promise. This promise of land and progeny is held up in the Old Testament as a remarkable gift of grace to Abraham and his descendants.

The Promised Land is always portrayed as a good land. When Moses talks about it after Israel's departure from Egypt he calls it a land "flowing with milk and honey" (Exod. 3.8, 17; 13.5; Lev. 20.24; Num. 13.27). Then when he nears the land from the east and tries to describe it to the Israelite tribes, he contrasts it with the land of Egypt. This will *not* be a place where irrigation (as in Nile systems) will be possible. This land will be a "land of hills and valleys, watered by the rain from the sky." Therefore it is a land under the direct care of God. It is "a land that the LORD your God looks after. The eyes of the LORD your God are always on it, from the beginning of the year to the end of the year" (Deut. 11.11–12).

While it will be a good land, it will not be an easy land. This will be a land that demands faith. Far from being paradise, this is a land that will hone a people. For instance, without a central river system, agriculture must rely on God, who supplies the land with water through rainfall. Culturally the land will not be empty but will be filled with Canaanites (and others) who will tempt Israel to compromise its unique commitment to God. And politically, armies moving from Egypt to Mesopotamia will run through this land as if it were a highway and Israel will be forced to decide whether its security will be found in local treaties and alliances or in God, who promises to sustain its welfare.

The Old Testament presents two "maps" of where this land is located. Numbers 34.1–12 defines this land as "the land of Canaan" extending from the Jordan river to the Mediterranean Sea (east to west) and from the "Brook of Egypt" to Hamath. These are the geographic parameters of ancient Canaan. This view is confirmed when Joshua 5.10–12 describes Israel's crossing of the Jordan as entry into "the land." Hence lands east of the Jordan river are excluded.

Deuteronomy 11.24 adds a larger expanse to the promise. It extends these boundaries and includes both sides of the Jordan (excluding Moab and Ammon) as well as northern reaches all the way to the Euphrates (so Gen. 15.18–21). Hence by this account, when Israel crosses the Arnon river (in Transjordan) its struggle for "the land" begins. This second map is viewed by many scholars as a later vision for political geography that may have come from the politically expansive era of the united monarchy.

But the center of this promise is certainly the hills west of the Jordan river. The promise focuses on the regions near Jerusalem, and when extended north and south, a claim can be made for the Promised Land that runs "from Dan to Beer-sheba" (Judg. 20.1).

The covenant and the land

In each reiteration of the promise, the land is linked to the covenant. For example, Genesis 17.8 records the land promise and this is followed in 17.9 with a reminder about covenant fidelity: "God said to Abraham, 'As for you, you shall keep my covenant, you and your offspring after you throughout their generations.'" In other words, the land is not a possession that may be enjoyed without reference to God. Possessing this land is contingent on Israel's ongoing faithfulness to God and obedience to his law. The land therefore is a byproduct of the covenant, a gift of the covenant. It is not a possession that can be held independently.

Both Leviticus and Deuteronomy warn Israel in stark terms about the conditional nature of this promise. Leviticus 18.24–30 warns about defilement with the culture of the Canaanites. If Israel embraces such unrighteousness, "the land will vomit you out for defiling it as it vomited out the nation that was before you." Leviticus 20.22–26 connects this theme to ritual holiness in the same way, "You shall keep all my statutes and all my ordinances, and observe them, so that the land to which I bring you to settle in may not vomit you out." The impression given is that the land itself can suffer abuse and be defiled. As sinners were ejected from the camp of Israel, so too, Israel can be ejected from the land of God.

Before Israel enters the land under Joshua's leadership, Deuteronomy records Moses' final words of encouragement and warning to the people.

> When you have had children and children's children, and become complacent in the land, if you act corruptly by making an idol in the form of anything, thus doing what is evil in the sight of the LORD your God, and provoking him to anger, I call heaven and earth to witness against you today that you will soon utterly perish from the land that you are crossing the Jordan to occupy; you will not live long on it, but will be utterly destroyed. The LORD will scatter you among the peoples; only a few of you will be left among the nations where the LORD will lead you.
>
> (Deut. 4.25–27)

The severity of these words is stunning. This land is not simply a gift the giver has forgotten. It is a gift that has expectations for covenant holiness and justice. God is watching this land. He has personal expectations for this land. It is a land that should evoke memories of his own holiness.

God's remarkable interest in this land can be explained by one undergirding theme. In a profound sense, Israel never "owns" the land of promise. *God owns this land.* Leviticus uses this idea to explain why the land cannot be sold permanently to others, "The land shall not be sold in perpetuity, *for the land is mine*; with me you are but aliens and tenants" (Lev. 25.23). Israel here is viewed as a tenant in this land, an alien, a renter. The recipient of a gift for use. But not a landlord. Israel must hold this land loosely, because God will determine the tenure of its occupants.

The Old Testament reinforces this notion of God's ownership of the land in a variety of ways. The land was not to be considered "private property," but was something distributed by God. The division of land was done by casting lots (Num. 26.55) thus making land use God's decision. The trustees of this use were the tribes, never individuals (Num. 36.3; Josh. 17.5). This "loose ownership" can be seen in the provisions for the jubilee year in Leviticus 25. No land could be bought or sold permanently – every 50th year the land had to return to the users God had declared in the beginning. God continues to exercise divine oversight to how this land is held.

Moreover the harvests of Israel were understood in light of God's ownership. First crops and first animals belonged to God and so were offered in sacrifice (Lev. 27.30–33; Deut. 14.22; 26.9–15). The command to "keep the Sabbath" was observed not only by Israel but by the land itself (Lev. 25.2). Here the land is personified as if it were living in a relationship with God, as if it too were living under covenant obligations.

Deuteronomy 12.9 refers to the land as a place of rest for Israel – but it is also a place of rest for God (Ps. 95.11; Isa. 66.1). "Resting place" refers to the place where God's presence dwells. In the wilderness narratives it is the place where God pauses (Num. 10.33) or dwells (Ps. 132.8).

Each of these themes underscores the same idea. This land is rightly called *holy land* because it belongs to a holy God (see Zech. 2.16, Heb. *'admat haqqodesh*). This land is *set apart*. No other land shares this quality. Other land is "unclean land" (Amos 7.17) and yet this land is his. Numbers 35.34 makes this explicit: "You shall not defile the land in which you live, in which I also dwell; for I the LORD dwell among the Israelites."

The possession and loss of land

The seriousness of living in the land of promise can be seen following Joshua's campaigns. He immediately takes the Israelite tribes north to the mountains of Ebal and Gerizim and requires that they recommit themselves to the covenant (Josh. 8.30–35). Following their breath-taking successes at Jericho and Ai, Israel's first duty is to renew loyalty to the covenant where their privileges of using the land are anchored. Joshua's rededication reinforces the idea (above) that covenant and land are inseparable and if land is held while the covenant is spurned, the warning read out on that day would fall on the nation.

The contingency of life in the land can be seen clearly in Judges, where each generation must work out the depth of their commitment to the covenant. And when their commitment fails, they experience the near-loss of tribal territory through war. At the end of the book, two troubling stories bring stark case-studies of this loss. The tribe of Dan indulges in breathtaking religious corruption (Judges 17—18) by instituting their own priesthood. Benjamin indulges in remarkable moral corruption (19—21) when a Levite's concubine is sexually abused and killed. In both cases, Dan and Benjamin put in jeopardy their privileges of living in the land. In each case, the theological message is the same: land and righteousness are inextricably linked.

The Old Testament continues with an array of stories showing how land-use and covenant righteousness cannot be separated. When David wishes to acquire land for God's temple in Jerusalem, he treats with righteousness Ornan the Jebusite (who owns the threshing floor David wants). This promised land, this land in Jerusalem, was owned by an "alien" and yet it "belonged" to Israel through promise. David does not take this land by force but purchases it at a steep price (600 shekels of gold, 1 Chronicles 21).

King Ahab presents the opposite position. He covets land in the verdant Jezreel valley held by a vineyard owner named Naboth. Ahab and Jezebel conspire to kill him in order to steal his land. And their unrighteousness is uncovered and condemned by none other than Elijah: "Have you killed and also taken possession?" (1 Kings 21.19). Rather than using Torah as an inspiration to righteousness, they use Torah in their plot to covet and steal. Covenant land cannot be taken by royal strategies of consumption.

The most dramatic example of land loss however appears in the Old Testament prophets. The prophet appears precisely in order to speak to Israel about land and its use, "When you come into the land…the LORD your God will raise up for you a prophet" (Deut.

18.9–15). This is because in the land where kings will rule, where land will be seen as an object of conquest, a commodity even, royalty must be reminded that they stand in relation to the land not as property/heir, but as gift/recipient. For the prophets, land is gift-land. Land is a place where covenant-righteousness must be on display. As Brueggemann explains, Israel failed to understand that it could not be a nation like other nations. Its king could not treat the land like other lands. This lesson was "the perennial lesson" that Israel had to learn – or else it would evolve into "the perennial temptation" of its national life.

Isaiah sounds these warnings sharply: "Ah, you who join house to house, who add field to field, until there is room for no one but you, and you are left to live alone in the midst of the land!" (Isa. 5.8). As does Micah: "Alas for those who devise wickedness and evil deeds on their beds! When the morning dawns, they perform it, because it is in their power. They covet fields, and seize them; houses, and take them away; they oppress householder and house, people and their inheritance" (Mic. 2.1–2). Virtually each of the prophets repeats the same warning given by Elijah to Ahab: murder and the misuse of land will be severely judged. This is true of Amos (4.1–2; 7.17), and Hosea (9.2–3). But perhaps this is most central to the devastating words of Jeremiah (3.19–20; 7.5–7). Voices will be heard in Ramah, lamentation and bitter weeping – Rachel is weeping for her children (Jer. 31.15). For Jeremiah the future of the nation's history is inevitable: it will lead to loss and exile. God himself will stir the king of Babylon ("my servant") to come against the land and devour it (25.8–9; 27.6).

Perhaps the most remarkable litany found among the prophets appears in Isaiah 5.1–7. This is Isaiah's famous Song of the Vineyard, which outlines God's vision for his people in the land. Israel would be like vines planted in a carefully tended vineyard. And all that the owner asks is that the vineyard yield good grapes. But alas, Isaiah announces, the owner is filled with despair: "And now, inhabitants of Jerusalem and people of Judah, judge between me and my vineyard. What more was there to do for my vineyard that I have not done in it? When I expected it to yield grapes, why did it yield wild grapes?" (Isa. 5.3–4). The ultimate consequence for this unrighteousness, this covenant betrayal, was complete land loss. "I will remove its hedge and it will be devoured."

This terror of land loss came to Judah in 586 BC in the form of Babylonian armies. Psalm 48 records the pride and over-confidence of Israel's view of land: it was a national possession guaranteeing divine privilege. Psalm 137 describes the shock and grief that swamped the nation when a Babylonian siege demolished Jerusalem's walls. The entire book of Lamentations wrestles with the confusion of the loss of promise, a loss that Israel had never imagined – that a life with Yahweh and a life in the land can come to an end (Hos. 9.17). But this is precisely the reality that the kings would not admit.

But for the prophets, land loss is also an avenue to renewal. Land loss is the necessary experience of faith within the covenant so that true obedience can be reclaimed. In a word, exiles will become new heirs. Therefore the prophets also point to a restoration of land (Amos 9.14–15; Hos. 2.14–23; 11.8–11; Jer. 16.15; Isa. 9.1–9). Following the exile a second entry to the land, almost a "second exodus," brings Israel back to the land-promise to reforge covenant faithfulness a second time. And once again for prophets such as Ezekiel and Malachi, land inheritance, covenant, and faithfulness must run together.

This closing and opening of a new chapter in the history of the land marked by the exile is poignantly given to us by Ezekiel. And it is Ezekiel who reinforces the rhythm of biblical faith's relationship to the land: gift of land promise, the obligations of land possession, and judgment leading to land loss. The land has been a gift and yet because Israel has despoiled this land, God's judgment must come upon it. "The end has come upon the four corners of the land" (7.2)! Moreover, the land itself is no longer a land that God can dwell in. His sanctuary has been defiled and as a result Israel's sin *has driven God out* (8.6). Thus God himself becomes an exile with Israel because the ruin of his land means that he cannot enjoy it either. The result? A desolation and a waste. "And I will make the land a desolation and a waste; and her proud might shall come to an end; and the mountains of Israel shall be so desolate that no one will pass through" (33.28).

But it is in Ezekiel that we also find hope. The renewal of Israel will be paralleled by the renewal of the land. Waste places will be rebuilt; desolate places replanted (36.33). And above all, God himself will return to the land and bring his glory in his return (43.1; 44.4). In chapters 47 and 48 this is symbolized by a return to the tribal distributions in Joshua. This is indeed a new beginning. But with a twist. The native-born aliens who live alongside Israel in the land should be treated as "citizens of Israel" (47.22). The alien will gain an inheritance alongside Israel (47.23) and the land will be shared in a way not imagined before.

After the exile

The return to the land after the exile is indeed a new beginning. Perhaps it should be viewed as a second exodus/conquest, a reclaiming of the land once more now with a clearer understanding of the obligations that accrue to those holding it. The infidelities and immoralities of the earlier period weighed on leaders like Ezra. The warnings and hope of the prophets were deeply familiar to them. They came to this era chastened and viewed this land that God had graciously given as impure, soiled by the sinfulness of another generation. "For we have disregarded your commandments!" (Ezra 9.10). Ezra goes as far as to describe the land as bearing the same impurity as that given by the Canaanites ("unclean with pollutions") and needing restoration. Therefore a religious intensity or sectarian exclusivity evolves with the return. Retaining the land is interpreted as embracing a strictly religious life.

To hold this land is to embrace the contingency of life there. Security depends on complete and utter loyalty to God's covenant. The land (according to Ezra) is not a re-conquest, it is a re-gifting, a new opportunity to live in a land set apart where God himself holds high standards of purity. This explains Ezra's strict prohibition on intermarriage with residents who do not share Israel's faith: it represents a compromise that will lead to the same land loss of earlier generations. Nehemiah likewise rails against those who were profaning the Sabbath. This too was a profound denial of covenant life, a sin that inevitably led to land loss.

The fortunes of Israel, from the fourth to the first centuries BC, only served to consolidate Judaism's commitment to the land. The memory of land loss and exile to Babylon did not dissipate with time. The threat was reinforced with new Hellenistic conquerors beginning with Alexander and his successors in Egypt and Syria. The land of Judea was a guarantee of survival, a foothold in history, a refuge in the mountains where safety could be found. And yet the seductions of Hellenistic life and the prosperity it offered led to more and more

Jews seeking their fortunes outside the country: Alexandria and Syrian Antioch, even coastal cities around the eastern Mediterranean gave birth to new, prosperous Jewish communities.

This new cultural assimilation into the all-consuming superculture of Hellenism posed an entirely new threat. This was a threat not of conquest, but of absorption. The enticement of different land and the endorsement of new cultural opportunities called to Israel from beyond its borders. And it forced an internal debate that continued right through the New Testament era. Is the Promised Land an ideal for Jewish life? Is it only a place of veneration and memory or should it be a genuine commitment for every member of the Jewish faith? Diaspora Judaism in the Hellenistic era raised a host of new questions. And as we shall see (Chapter 4), these questions from the Diaspora brought shocking responses to the leaders of Judea both before and after the great war of AD 70.

One of the major contributions of W. D. Davies' seminal work, *The Gospel and the Land*, is his analysis of the Jewish discussion about the land throughout the Hellenistic period.[2] The new Jewish literature penned during this time sounded all of the same notes known in the Old Testament. The Land of Promise is holy and good (Wisd. 13.3; *Jubilees* 13.2) and deeply valued by God (Wisd. 13.4–7). The *Psalms of Solomon* summarize the work of the coming Messiah thus: "He shall gather together a holy people whom he will lead in righteousness; and he shall distribute them according to their tribes upon the land. And the alien and the foreigner will no longer live with them" (17.26–28). The eschatological privilege of Israel will be gaining land and no longer having to endure the cultural encroachments of Hellenistic life.

And while Israel's privilege of having the land is granted, it is always anchored in the covenant where the promise is confirmed (*Jubilees* 22.27). But if this is true, the contingency of this land-possession is also sounded. Davies reminds us, "In Jub 6.12–13, failure to observe the demands of Yahweh is incompatible with occupation of The Land."[3] The reward of obeying the law and remaining faithful to covenant is – according to *Jubilees* 15.28 – that Israel will not be "rooted out of the land."

In Jewish end-time expectation (apocalyptic) the land plays a prominent role not as the seat of judgment but as a place of refuge. Surviving the great and devastating events of the Day of the Lord can be assured if one lives in the land (*4 Ezra* 9.7–9; 13.48). In this sense, the land can come to Israel's rescue (*4 Ezra* 71.1) because it will work on behalf of God preserving his people.

The Dead Sea Scrolls found near Qumran represent a stark variation on Israel's territorial holdings. While Qumran validates the preciousness and goodness of the land, still, these sectarians believed that the land itself continued to be weighed down by impurity. Their removal to the desert where a "way in the wilderness" might be built is predicated on the hopelessness of the Hasmonean empire being built in Jerusalem. Their concern is that the same divine judgment that fell in the sixth century might return due to unrighteousness. Therefore calls to purity prevail (1QS 1.5) and reminders to covenant faithfulness are common so that Israel will not lose the land (1QS 8.3).

The unexpected development is that the community sees itself pursuing righteousness for the sake of the nation. They are making *atonement for the land* (1QS 8.10; 9.3). The rigors of Qumran life are compensating for the sins of Jerusalem and its compromised Temple. Qumran is a remnant, a righteous few whose fidelity to the law will contribute to God's ongoing commitment to his promises. The War Scroll reinforces this theme with preparations for a final battle where not only will the land be purged of Gentile influence, but righteous Israel will prosecute a war beyond the boundaries of the land so that the source of all impurity will cease.

To sum, the same themes sounded in the Old Testament continue into the Jewish era. The land is central to Jewish identity; the promise of the land is anchored to the covenant; and life in the land is contingent on upholding the righteousness expected by God.

The rabbis: reinforcing commitments

The volatile first century both before and after the war of AD 66–70 continues Israel's timeless conversation about land and religious identity. The tripartite formula of land, God and Israel is reinforced again and again by many of Jerusalem's rabbis. The liturgies and prayers of Judaism point regularly to the land. The Eighteen Benedictions (a late-first-century synagogue liturgy) provide a corporately recited call for blessing of the land and life in it. Benediction 18: "Bestow your peace upon Israel and upon your people and upon your city and upon your inheritance [= land]; And bless us, all of us together.

Blessed are you, O Lord, who makes peace." This is a remarkable prayer when we consider that at its writing, Jerusalem was a ruin, the Temple had been burned and the land had been devastated by multiple Roman legions.

The Mishnah (Judaism's oral laws, compiled in about AD 200) points to these concerns about the land and no doubt must be read as a reaction to many Jews who left the war-torn country for other more tranquil places around the Mediterranean. Should Jews farming in far-off Syria pay tithes? Is there benefit to being buried in the land in order to enjoy the resurrection to come? And how might the law be applied to a Diaspora Jew if the law was intended for application to the land? Fully 30 percent of the Mishnah prescribes guidance which can only be practiced within the land. And despite the shocking losses incurred during the first war with Rome – and even the devastating losses witnessed with Bar Kokhba in AD 135 – still, many in Judea held on to its unyielding attachment to the land. After Bar Kokhba, a rabbinic discourse belonging to Rabbi Simeon b. Yohai provided comments on Habbakuk 3.6, "He rose and measured the earth."

> R. Simeon b. Yohai opened a discourse with this: "He rose and measured the earth" [Hab. 3.6]. The Holy One, blessed by He, considered all generations and he found no generation fitted to receive the Torah other than the generation of the wilderness; the Holy One, blessed be He, considered all mountains and found no mountain on which the Torah should be given other than Sinai; the Holy One, blessed by He, considered all cities, and found no city wherein the Temple might be built, other than Jerusalem; the Holy One, blessed be He, considered all lands, and found no land suitable to be given to Israel, other than the Land of Israel. This is indicated by what is written: "He rose and measured the earth."
>
> (*Leviticus Rabbah* 13.2)[4]

In this and numerous other rabbinic sayings the centrality and sanctity of life in the land is unavoidable. And no doubt this is reinforced by the obligation to engage in religious sacrifice and worship in the land. The Mishnah records, "There are ten degrees of holiness. The Land of Israel is holier than any other land. Wherein lies its holiness? In that from it they may bring the *omer* [offering], the first fruits, the two loaves, which they may not bring from any other land" (*Kelim* 1.6–9).

In a commentary on Numbers 34.2, we learn about correct blessings during meals:

> Of all the blessings there is none more precious than the one, "For the land and for the food." For our rabbis have said that any one who does not mention in the grace after meals the blessing, "for the land and for the food," has not fulfilled his duty. The Holy One, blessed be He, said, "The land of Israel is more precious to me than everything."
>
> *(Numbers Rabbah* 23.7)

But Jewish voices in this period were not necessarily uniform (see Chapter 2). Of course, Diaspora Judaism that had put down roots in places like Alexandria, Syrian Antioch and Ephesus might have vigorously disagreed with this exclusive claim on the Promised Land. The Diaspora's culturally liberal approach to Jewish life is directly connected to the anxiety felt about the entire project of Hellenization that Judaism was experiencing. Nevertheless, despite the freedom desired by the Diaspora, the liturgies of Judaism and the history of its faith pulled Jews back to the Land of Promise. Diaspora synagogues were eager to have their festival calendars fixed by those in Jerusalem. To observe the Day of Atonement on the incorrect day would be unforgivable. Further, following AD 70 Jewish synagogues both in the land and in the Diaspora began praying in the direction of Jerusalem and its lost Temple – a practice still observed commonly today.

Another window into Diaspora attachment to the land comes from archaeology. Jewish burial in the land was desired and possible for Diaspora Jews (preferably on the Mount of Olives) until Hadrian prohibited it in AD 135. Then interest moved to Galilee, where the village of Beit She'arim became prominent. Rabbi Judah HaNasi (135–217), the great compiler of the Mishnah, not only lived there but after his death in Sepphoris, he was buried in Beit She'arim alongside countless Hellenistic Jews who believed that at least burial in the land brought blessing.[5]

Summary

These many sources trace a continuous line from the Old Testament through the Mishnah. The land had become a place of supreme religious commitment which only intensified with the cultural threat of Hellenism and the political losses under Rome. Conversation about the land was continuous and vigorous right through the New Testament era. And therefore as we open its pages, despite its apparently muted interest in the land, we can easily suppose that this conversation was known and weighed by Jesus and his followers from the beginning.

Jewish commitment to the land never disappeared – though in the Diaspora it was debated as we shall see. Despite the heated rhetoric between Palestinians and Jews today where in some cases Arabs have tried to deny Jewish life in the land following Bar Kokhba (135), there is ample evidence that some minimal form of Jewish life continued in the land for 2,000 years – just as Arab life has continued there for the same length of time. Jewish presence in Jerusalem may have been minimal. But in Galilee at Tiberius or Sepphoris or Safed it was considerable. Until the great migrations of Jews from Europe began arriving in the late nineteenth century, Jewish life, even in its fragmented state, continued to hold to the land as a religious duty.

· · ·

2

Diaspora Judaism and the land

Both Christian and Jewish identification with the land were in a formative stage in the first century and experiencing considerable redefinition. As we have seen, Jewish life in Judea was unflinching in its territorial commitments and this led not only to strict expectations for Jewish life within the land but exasperation with foreign occupiers. In some respects, religious territoriality spilled into nationalism but clearly the two (religion and nation) cannot be separated. Roman Judea was a religious state. Its national program was buttressed by its religious commitments.

But a new problem emerged in the Hellenistic period. What would Judaism think about those lands nearby where Jews might live? And what about those cities – the major Decapolis cities for example – where Hellenism had been deeply entrenched for centuries? In the Maccabean period their conquest and suppression were deemed vital. And in some cases, Jewish leaders tried to impose Jewish culture on them (rather as the Greeks had done to them). In the second century BC, the Jewish ruler Alexander Jannaeus conquered the Decapolis cities of east Galilee and Syria and demanded that they submit to his rule. They obliged. But when he came to the magnificent city of Pella resting on hills due east from Scythopolis (beyond the Jordan river), he destroyed it because, as Josephus notes, "the city would not adopt Jewish customs" (*Antiquities*, 13.395–397).

However, another problem came from a different quarter. What about those lands beyond Judea's reach? For hundreds of years, Jews had migrated to regions throughout the Mediterranean. Archaeological work is providing evidence of Jewish life in these distant cities. In 1981 in Plovdiv (central Bulgaria) a Jewish synagogue was discovered attached to the ancient city of Philippopolis giving proof of Judaism's wide distribution even here.[1] Another synagogue with evidence of first-century remains has now been found in Ostia, the port of Rome.

15

Elsewhere in Italy ancient Jewish communities are evidenced in Puteoli, Pompeii, Venosa, and Naples.[2]

This dispersal (the Septuagint refers to it as a *diaspora*, or scattering) of Jewish life into non-Jewish cities in the Roman empire raised questions about the integrity of Jewish identity outside the land. *Is it legitimate to be a Jew and live in places like Corinth? Are not sincere Jews obligated to live in the Holy Land?* Earlier scholarship once described Diaspora Judaism as compromised by Hellenism and not normative. But abundant evidence now makes clear that these Diaspora communities saw themselves as fully Jewish, holding to their culture and faith with integrity. Nevertheless the question remains: What about the land? Had Diaspora Judaism rethought the relationship between religious faith and Holy Land?

This last question is not peripheral for the history of early Christian identity and the New Testament. The earliest church was Jewish, well aware of debates about the land, and as we will see, likely shaped by attitudes formed in Diaspora Judaism.

The Jewish Diaspora and the land

Jews generally left Judea and arrived in the Diaspora for one of two reasons. Either they were conquered and taken as slaves or they moved voluntarily, looking for greater opportunities. Mesopotamia tells the story well. Forced removals of the Jews from Judea began with the Babylonian exile in the sixth century BC. Within a few hundred years, the Jewish Diaspora in the east had large and significant Jewish communities in Babylonia, Parthia, Media, and Armenia. Years later Antiochus III saw this growth and could force the removal of 2,000 Jewish families from Mesopotamia and move them to Lydia and Phrygia in Asia Minor (*Antiquities*, 12.145–153). Josephus says that in his day two cities near Babylon, Nisibis and Nehardea, were the center of Jewish life there (*Antiquities*, 18.310–313, 379).[3] The conversion of Queen Helena of Adiabene (on the Tigris river), whose tomb still stands north of Jerusalem's old city, is further evidence of a lively Jewish life in Mesopotamia. By the first century, Josephus could refer to the impressive size and importance of the Jewish communities in the east. On the remote stretches of the Euphrates river in north Syria, the Dura-Europas synagogue illustrates Jewish life near this period and has given to scholarship the earliest pictorial representation of Jews we possess.[4]

In the east, Jewish communities were also drawn to Syria. Not only were cities like Damascus and Antioch (on the Orontes river) nearby, but Syrian kings such as Seleucus I Nicator (358–281 BC) gave financial incentives to Jews to move north. By the first century, the Jews in Syria outnumbered all other populations (Josephus, *Wars*, 7.43–53). The Jewish community in Syrian Antioch was hundreds of years old by the first century, notably large, and successful (*Antiquities*, 12.119–124; *Wars*, 7.43–53). A glimpse of its size comes from a grim source, however. During the war of AD 66–70, Josephus says in one passage that 10,000 Jews were massacred in Syrian Antioch (*Wars*, 2.561) and in another the count is 18,000 (*Wars*, 7.368). Both numbers are no doubt exaggerated but nevertheless they point to a significant Jewish population center there.

A similar story of Jewish settlement could be told for Egypt, where Philo puts an estimate of the number of Jews there at 1 million (*Flaccus*, 43). Some Jews fled to Egypt during the devastating sixth-century BC conquest (Jer. 43.6–7). Over the next five centuries Jews were forcibly moved there or migrated voluntarily. By the first century, two of Alexandria's five residential sectors were Jewish (Philo, *Flaccus*, 8).

Awareness of the extent of the known world west of Judea and its populations can be found in Jewish writing from the period. Josephus, for example, provides a speech of King Agrippa I at the beginning of his *Jewish Wars* (2.345–401), where he details how Rome rules the entire earth. He then supplies an impressive table of nations that Rome has defeated, no doubt to persuade Jewish rebels still holding dreams of revolt. As a catalogue it gives us some idea of how a first-century Jew understood his world.

Philo supplies a valuable perspective on a first-century under-standing of the Diaspora in his *Embassy to Gaius*. Here he quotes an alleged letter to the Emperor Gaius sent by King Agrippa I (*Embassy*, 276–329). The letter is an appeal that the emperor not plunder the Jerusalem Temple because of its sanctity to so many citizens within the empire. Then Philo provides a distinctive Jewish perspective on the globe – which even omits Italy and Rome. Philo lists the many cities where Jews live within the empire and argues that Jerusalem is indeed the universal capital (Greek, *metropolis*) of all these people. Thus any benefit distributed to Jerusalem would actually benefit cities everywhere. Where are these Jewish colonies found? Agrippa points to Europe, Asia, and Libya; in all of the islands of the

Mediterranean; and along both coastlands and inland. His point: Jews are everywhere.

Gathering up these sources demonstrates that the size of the western Diaspora was truly impressive. Agrippa's letter to the Emperor Gaius provides some of the details. In addition to Syria, Phoenicia, and Egypt, Philo mentions Jews in Asia Minor (Bithynia, Pontus, Pamphylia, Cilicia) and regions west: Thessalonica, Boeotia, Macedonia, Aetolia, Attica, Argos, Corinth, and the Peloponnesus. But archaeological and literary evidence point to yet more communities too numerous to list. Among them, Rome is the most prominent. Josephus tells how Pompey brought Jewish captives here in 63 BC (*Antiquities*, 14.79), and by 59 BC Cicero reports that they were a respected, secure community (*Pro Flacco*, 28.66–67). By the first century both pagan and Jewish writers can speak of the large Roman Jewish community with great specificity. Inscriptions in Rome's Jewish catacombs (second to fourth centuries) refer to 11 and possibly 13 synagogues in the city. It is no surprise to hear Josephus quoting proudly from Strabo (85 BC) about his own Jewish people: "This people has already made its way into every city and it is not easy to find any place in the inhabited world which has not received this nation and in which it has not made its power felt" (*Antiquities*, 14.115).

The influential city of Sardis in western Asia Minor demonstrates the rich and esteemed life Jews could enjoy. Josephus mentions Jewish life there frequently and even notes that the Jewish community sponsored its own civil court so that Jews who were Roman citizens could bypass the usual imperial legal systems (*Antiquities*, 14.235). Abundant inscriptional evidence of Sardis' Jews has now been surpassed by the recovery of a synagogue complete with a large bath, a gymnasium complex dating to the first century, and over 80 inscriptions.[5]

It is impossible to know how many Jews lived in the Diaspora. Some have argued for Rome's Jewish population at 40,000. Others speculate that the entire Diaspora numbered anywhere from 4 to 6 million. Still others think that Jews comprised 10 percent of the empire itself. If 4 million lived in the western Diaspora and 1 million in Egypt, estimates are that Judea's population was about 3 million. For our interest, one aspect of these numbers is vital: *more Jews were living outside the Holy Land than were living in it.* And this brought major implications to Jewish thinking and perspective.

Fidelity and separation

It is impossible to imagine a Jewish family living in the Roman empire which did not have some degree of affection for the land of Judea. The liturgies of Jewish worship and particularly the cycle of festival celebration constantly reminded the Diaspora Jew that his or her roots were located in Judea. Still the Jewish challenge was what we might term "boundary maintenance." To what extent should Roman culture be kept out in order to maintain authentic Jewish identity? There was likely a range of assimilation into Roman life and habits within Diaspora Judaism and no generalization can represent the entire story.[6] But no doubt as one maintained this "boundary" there was an immediate effect on loyalty to the land.

Fidelity to traditional Jewish commitments was reinforced by numerous shared experiences that unified the Jewish Diaspora. Sabbath observance, dietary law, and circumcision contributed to building markers of Jewish identity and communal life. Philo describes it thus: "On Sabbath days in all the cities thousands of houses of learning were opened, in which discernment and moderation and proficiency and righteous living and indeed all virtues were taught" (*Special Laws*, 2.62).[7] This likely explains why Jewish communities lived in districts within their cities (*Antiquities*, 14.259–261). Such arrangements were a by-product of cultural cohesion.

The Jerusalem Temple also remained as a significant place of affection and reinforced commitment to the land (Philo, *Embassy to Gaius*, 184–185). The *Letter of Aristeas*, penned a century before the New Testament, describes in detail a visit to Jerusalem, where the Temple is "characterized by a grandeur and costliness truly unprecedented" (*Aristeas*, 85; see 83–120). Tied to this was pilgrimage to Jerusalem for festivals. As Philo says, "Multitudes from countless cities come, some overland, others over the sea, from east and west and north and south at every feast" (*Special Laws*, 1.69). Josephus exaggerates the numbers of pilgrims swelling Jerusalem during festivals (he counts 2.7 million! *Wars*, 6.425), but this likely just underscores the significance of the seasonal migration.

Fidelity to the land was also assured through the annual Temple tax. Philo gives a full description of how storehouses were kept in each Jewish Diaspora community and groups of leaders were nominated to escort it to Jerusalem each year (*Special Laws*, 1.76–78).

The amount of money moving to Judea became so huge that some Romans wanted to legislate against or limit it while other unscrupulous rulers simply stole it from regional storage houses. At one point, the Roman general Crassus (d. 53 BC) aimed to rob the Temple to finance his war in Parthia, and a priest offered him a gold bar worth 10,000 shekels. Crassus took it then looted the Temple of the rest of its gold (*Antiquities*, 14.109–110). Even after the fall of the Temple in AD 70, this money continued to come to Judea and was collected by displaced Jewish leaders (the "patriarchate") who continued to receive it even till the fourth century.[8]

Therefore many Diaspora Jews lived with a heartfelt commitment to the land reinforced with ceremonies and contributions. Perhaps many believed with Philo that indeed Jerusalem was the capital not only of Judea "but of many other lands" due to the many Jews living there (*Embassy to Gaius*, 281). Another sign of this commitment was the desire of many Diaspora Jews to be buried in the land. The massive cemetery/necropolis in southern Galilee's Beit Shear'im holds 20 catacombs with countless graves pointing to this quest.

Nevertheless, the fact remains that these Jews did *not* choose to live in Judea. They had accommodated themselves in vast numbers to the diversity of the empire. Their affection for the land was evident in their religious life but they also maintained a cultural investment in Hellenism that made them less like the Jews in the province of Judea. Signs of this can be seen in their thoroughgoing use of Greek and their adoption of Greek names. Even the frescoes at Dura Europas display both Aramaic and Greek scripts – along with Hellenistic attire. In Alexandria, the Jews held an annual festival on the island of Pharos (home of the famed lighthouse) celebrating the translation of the Scriptures into Greek (Philo, *Life of Moses*, 2.41–42). This translation is called the Septuagint (derived from the Latin for "seventy", abbreviated LXX) and it took its name from a legend that 72 Jewish scholars had translated the Hebrew Scriptures into Greek identically, thus showing God's endorsement of the project. Texts record Jewish attendance at Roman games, athletics, and public shows as well as schools. They acquired citizenship and married Gentiles. Even the use of figurative animal and human images in art show this investment in Hellenistic culture. The little-known Hellenistic Jewish author Artapanus models this cultural syncretism well. In his legend (surviving only as fragments) he tells how Moses and the Patriarchs not only began Judaism but started all world civilizations, even the Egyptian polytheistic cults.[9]

Perhaps their most profound accommodation to Hellenism was their willingness to use allegorical interpretations for their Scriptures. Here the particularities of Jewish ritual became symbol and a literal obedience to the law took on new meaning. As we shall see, Philo does this very thing for the land promises of Israel. Diaspora communities also developed liturgies for use during the festival seasons such as Passover and Tabernacles when travel to the Temple was impossible – or after the Temple no longer existed. The Mishnah gives set texts that could be studied *away from Jerusalem* during these seasons (*Megillah* 3.5–6).

The furthest extent of this theological separation is illustrated by the Jewish temple built at Leontopolis in Egypt. In the second century BC, Onias IV, a Jewish man of priestly lineage, came to Egypt because of lost prospects of becoming high priest in Jerusalem (*Wars*, 7.426–432). He was given an abandoned pagan temple by Ptolemy VI and rebuilt it as a replica of the Jerusalem Temple – claiming this had been prophesied by Isaiah. Soon Jewish priests were offering sacrifices and celebrating the festivals. This practice continued after the destruction of Jerusalem when the Romans finally shut it down (AD 73). Of course Jerusalem never acknowledged this temple and most Egyptian Jews ignored it. Still it is a remarkable phenomenon on the Jewish Diaspora landscape.

The land redefined

Diaspora Judaism was willing to make an accommodation therefore to a world of ethnic diversity, where life as a minority was acceptable and where the practice of Jewish life and faith was not compromised by living outside Judea. And this Diaspora numbered in the millions. For them the reality of life in the land often became eschatological. In prayer and worship they imagined a time when one day all Judaism would return to the land and it would be free of its poverty and wars. The early writings of Ben Sirach (36.11), Tobit (13.3), and 2 Maccabees (2.18) promote this eschatological dream. Closer to the New Testament period, the *Psalms of Solomon* prays, "Bring together the dispersed of Israel with goodness and mercy" (8.28; cf. 11.1–4). And in the first century, Philo can say the same when Israel will leave this "exile" of

Diaspora and return "home" – but as we will see, this may well be an allegory for him (*On Rewards*, 162–172).[10] But this dream would be for another era, an eschatological time when God's rule would dominate and when the surrounding pagan cultures would be kept at bay. It was not a prescription for how life might be lived in the present. Certainly the shocking devastation of Judea in AD 66–70 questioned that hope and forced Diaspora Jews to rethink the costliness of a theology linked to Judea and the practical value of living elsewhere.

We have firm evidence that at least two leading Diaspora writers were well underway rethinking the meaning of the land for Jewish faith. In a valuable essay, Betsy Halpern Amaru has provided a window into how both Philo and Josephus redefined the land.[11] In each case Amaru looks at how these men interpreted the land in four categories: (1) the Patriarchal promises and covenant; (2) the unique properties of the land; (3) Torah legislation and the land; and (4) messianism. In each case, what Philo and Josephus do is astounding.

Philo is inspired by his desire to adapt Judaism to Hellenistic thought and he does this by allegorizing his Bible. For him, the truth of the concrete objects of Jewish life now take on a new meaning. *The land is reinterpreted as the knowledge and wisdom of God.* Thus he neglects the land promises found in Abraham and the patriarchs whenever the covenant is mentioned. No land promise appears even in discussions of Isaac or Jacob. In Genesis 28.10–22 when Jacob dreams at Bethel, the Hebrew text's explicit reaffirmation of the land promise (28.13) is replaced by Philo with a promise of wisdom and virtue. The promise that Joseph would be buried in the Promised Land in Philo becomes a hope that his soul will inhabit "cities of virtue." Canaan becomes not a place of religious promise but a metaphor, a stage of development for the soul. Moses' leadership, therefore, will not take Israel to the Promised Land, but to a higher level of maturity and wisdom. Even in his eschatology, Philo does not see a *literal* ingathering of exiled Israel to a literal Promised Land. This instead will be an arrival into a state of deeper wisdom. As Amaru concludes, "In Philo, this Judaism is described as a religious or cultural 'nationality' minimally tied to a single ethnic base or territory."[12]

Josephus is inspired by different ideas but arrives at a similar destination. Having witnessed the great war with Rome, Josephus is eager to make Jewish faith and culture palatable to Roman sensibilities for pragmatic reasons. For him, a religiously fired Jewish territoriality led to rebellion, brought war, and ruined Judaism's public respect within the empire. Therefore in *The Antiquities* when Josephus cites the covenant promises, he too neglects the land. The blessing promised to Israel is *greatness*, but the land is not a divine gift. Thus Abraham migrates to Canaan on his own inspiration – not in response to a divine promise of land. Likewise when Jacob dreams at Bethel, the promise of God is not for the land but for gracious aid and blessing (*Antiquities*, 1.272). Even in the conquest of Canaan, any sense of "promised land" is missing (*Antiquities*, 1.235).

Absent from Josephus are any of the romantic portrayals of the land as perfect or holy and divinely protected. The land is simply "favorable" (*Antiquities*, 2.296). When the Torah is described by him, the gift of land forms neither an incentive nor a warning. The common phrase in Deuteronomy, "When you come into the land…" suddenly disappears in Josephus. When Moses gives the Torah at Sinai, Josephus retells the blessings that accrue to those who obey, "for if you will follow [the law], you will lead a happy life and you will enjoy the land fruitful, the sea calm, and the fruit of the womb born complete, as nature requires" (*Antiquities*, 3.88). The difference between this recounting and the story in Exodus is telling (12.25; 13.5; 20.12; 23.23–33; 34.11). The land as covenant promise is absent.

Clearly Josephus has altered an important feature of his people's story. He is eager to step away from a rigid territorialism he knew so well in earlier years. And when he writes at the end of the first century, he recreates biblical history in a manner favorable to Diaspora Judaism and Rome. He wants nothing to do with the religiously inspired Zealot land-claims from the war. His God is a universal God – and all lands live under God's providence.

Summary

What has happened here? In both Philo and Josephus the Jewish people now have become an esteemed cultural or religious "nationality" in the Roman world.[13] They are a people widely distributed through-out the empire *without a necessary territorial base*. The benefit of life within their ranks is not an eschatological promise of the defeat of the Gentiles and the resumption of an Israelite kingdom. Nor will blessing be found in the land given as reward. Instead, obedience to God within the Jewish framework will result in a better life, longevity, even prosperity.

Here then we see that Judaism's "Land Theology" has been entirely redefined. And it will be a redefinition that will deeply influence the formation of Christian thinking in the New Testament.

3

Jesus and the land

In the mid-40s of the first century, territorial nationalism in Judea began to boil over. Josephus tells us about a man named Theudas who lived under the Roman procurator Fadus. And Theudas had decided to wed armed resistance to a religious vision for the land of Judea (*Antiquities*, 20.5.1; cf. Acts 5.33–39). This land belonged to the Jews, Theudas argued, and it needed to be cleansed of those Gentiles who occupied it. Theudas took 400 men to the Jordan river, claimed a Joshua-like re-entry that would reconquer the land, and decided he would defeat Rome as if they were the new Canaanites. The procurator Fadus would have none of it. His cavalry met the Jewish rebels in the desert, killed them, captured Theudas, and brought his head to Jerusalem as a trophy.

Two years later Rome's next procurator, Alexander, began re-registering Judea for tax purposes. Again, violent resistance erupted. Josephus describes a man named Judas the Galilean who saw this act as so offensive that he was willing to die in war to stop it (*Antiquities*, 20.5.2; cf. 18.1.6). If the land were to provide revenue, it belonged to Israel and the Temple, not a Gentile occupier. God was the only ruler of the land and any who claimed sovereign rule usurped his role. The Romans quickly and easily killed Judas as well as his sons, and this stood as a second warning to the Jews about who owned the land.

These two stories provide a convenient window into the nationalistic tensions at work in first-century Judea. Ownership and control of the land by the Jews had been frustrated since the Roman conquest in 63 BC. The great accomplishments of the Maccabees in the second century BC driving Greek occupiers from the Judean mountains and establishing a Jewish kingdom had now been lost to Rome. Theologies of land restoration – yearnings for a new and successful era of Jewish sovereignty over its ethnic heritage – were everywhere in the wind.

25

Even the New Testament points to these aspirations. In Acts 1.6 the apostles ask Jesus a seemingly innocent question: "Lord, is this the time when you will restore the kingdom to Israel?" Now that the power of Jesus has been seen in his resurrection, their assumptions are clear. This messianic power must conclude with the fulfillment of Israel's vision. Jesus had spoken about the kingdom – did this not include the kingdom of Israel? The land would be returned to its rightful owners. The current exile, a Gentile exile as dreadful as that in Babylon, should end. A Jewish kingdom would prevail and Rome would leave.

The same frustrated hope is recorded in Luke 24.21. In despair the disciples at Emmaus tell the unrecognized resurrected Jesus that their dreams had been dashed at the cross. "We had hoped that he was the one to redeem Israel." This desire fits well with the stresses felt throughout the country. Redemption would come only when the land itself would be returned to the Jews and the foreign occupation ended. "Redeeming Israel" does not refer to the salvation of souls, but to the restoration of the nation, the cleansing of the land, and a divinely endorsed inheritance of the Holy Land that was deeply woven into the fabric of Israel's religious life.

If such concerns about Jewish identity and the land were widespread in early first-century Judea, Jesus was surely aware of these debates and their competing visions. A faith centered on Torah, Temple, and land could not ignore the problem of occupation. Jesus' contemporaries knew three alternatives that witnessed regular debate: cooperation, separation, or resistance. One could cooperate with the occupation and hope that Rome would ease its control and the imperial demands would relax over time. And who knows, perhaps the province could even benefit from Augustus' *Pax Romana*. Why not try to make it work? Herod and his dynasty had pursued this model fully. Any Roman ship arriving at the famed port of Caesarea Maritima in Judea was greeted not only by state-of-the-art anchorage with marble quays and tapestry awnings, but an expansive marble temple for Augustus loomed over the breakwater. Roman public architecture, a theater seating 3,500, and a hippodrome hosting 20,000 spectators for horse or chariot racing, confirmed loudly that this was a *Roman* port. Judea had never seen anything like this. Herod modeled the cooperative outlook on the Roman occupation. Even two of Herod's sons, Herod Antipas and Philip (by his wife Cleopatra), were educated in Rome (*Antiquities*, 17.20).

On the other hand one could separate from this wretched occupation and build an alternate community where believers could pray for relief and await God's intervention. The sectarians of Qumran near the Dead Sea pursued this course. Jerusalem and the land had become intolerably unclean not only through the Romans but through those Jews who were running Jerusalem and flirting with the occupiers. Life in the land had become impossible. In the wilderness where purity was still possible they prepared a place for the Lord. And for them an eschatological solution brought resolution. Qumran's *War Scroll* outlined how God would bring about his own intervention and the task of the believer was waiting and preparing. Its opening lines (1QM1.1–7) lay out the contours of the final battle between the "sons of light" and the "sons of darkness." The opponents are the Kittim (a frequent code for the Romans) and Jews who have ignored the life of righteousness by aligning themselves with the "sons of darkness."

Or one could resist by refusing to pay taxes or even by taking up the sword. If Judas Maccabeus had done it in the second century BC, why couldn't Israel be successful again? We might call this a reborn "Maccabean Vision" – a religiously fired Jewish nationalism that saw its first order of business as the cleansing of the land. This was no doubt the vision of Judas the Galilean and Theudas. And it is echoed in the messianic *Psalms of Solomon*: "Wisely and righteously let him [Messiah] expel sinners from *the inheritance*, and destroy the sinner's pride as a potter's vessel. With a rod of iron may he break in pieces all their resources. Let him destroy the lawless Gentiles by the word of his mouth" (17.21–24). But this was a dangerous vision that ultimately led to the destruction of Jerusalem and the devastation of the nation by war. Indeed the land was "cleansed" – but Rome did the cleansing with its own legions by devastating Judaism beyond repair.

Do the Gospels give us any insight into Jesus' attitudes?

Land and politics in Jesus' world

In the volatile climate of first-century politics – among a people living under the harsh realities of the Roman military occupation – we should not expect a public teacher like Jesus to speak explicitly about the land and its rightful owners. To exhibit resistance to Rome is to run up against a skilled army which is watching for signs of subversion. To show cooperation with Rome is to run up against fellow Jews for whom such sympathies are intolerable. In every explosive political context (both today and in antiquity), people with opinions must remain opaque to the many listeners standing in the shadows who are choosing sides.

When W. D. Davies wrote *The Gospel and the Land* in 1974, he was keenly aware of the old thesis that had been renewed by S. G. F. Brandon in 1967.[1] In *Jesus and the Zealots*, Brandon argued not only that Jesus objected to the political occupation of Rome, but that he was publicly sympathetic with a movement called the Zealots who advocated open resistance. However, the evangelists, who wrote their Gospels following the war of 66–70, were eager to cooperate with the empire, disassociate themselves from recalcitrant Judaism, and tame Jesus' image as a political activist. Thus Brandon discerned multiple layers in the Gospel tradition that betrayed not only the evangelists' correction but the truer, authentic portrait of a fully political Jesus.

Since 1967, Brandon's thesis has not won the day despite efforts of scholars such as J. D. Crossan.[2] His critical reconstruction of Jesus may owe as much to the 1960s and its political and social upheavals as it does to an honest exegesis of Gospel texts. From the early work of Davies to the more recent efforts of N. T. Wright,[3] a new portrait has emerged that has added nuance and complexity to Jesus' view of the land. Indeed politics and land claims were a potent religious force in the first century; but Jesus' relationship to them held an allusive subtlety that requires close examination.

Two initial observations deserve attention. First, Jesus is surprisingly silent with regard to the territorial aspirations and politics of his day. The national ambitions of Judaism under Rome constantly pressed Jewish leadership to respond. Either Judea was capitulating to the occupation or Judea had to organize to defeat it. However, Jesus is oddly silent about the debate. Moreover Jesus is curiously receptive to contact with the occupiers. In Matthew 8.5–13, he responds to the request of a Roman centurion whose valued servant was ill. Here we find no repulsion of the soldier, no condemnation of Gentiles, but rather we find receptivity and welcome. He says of the Roman: "Not even in Israel have I found such faith" (8.10). What emerges is a general impression that Israel's national ambitions tied to reclaiming the land live on the margin of Jesus' thinking.

There was a Roman law (now well known) that if a Roman soldier wanted a defeated subject to be his porter, he could demand it. This rule included use of the person's donkey and cart as well. But the law limited this service to one (Roman) mile. Although this provision for forced labor was deeply resented, in Matthew 5.41 Jesus announces that if you are told to go one mile in such a situation, *go two miles*! And he says more. In 5.44 he commands his followers to love "their enemies" and pray for those who persecute them. These are certain allusions to the Roman occupation that not only deny political resistance but were no doubt inexplicable to Jesus' followers. In a word, Jesus is strangely unsympathetic to attitudes that would demand resistance to Rome and the struggle for the land as religious duties.

However, in an important passage, Jesus is tested by those who chose aggressive resistance.

Following the removal of the corrupt and violent Archelaus (son of Herod I) in AD 6, the subsequent political disruption that brought direct Roman rule to the land inspired new forms of Jewish resistance. Instability and reorganization in AD 6 presented an ideal opportunity for this agenda.

For many Jews Roman taxation had become a burdensome symbol of Israel's enslavement and it was widely believed that it was the basis of Judea's financial value to the empire. In AD 6, tax revolts sought to lessen this value. Mark 12.13–17 records Jesus confronted by "Pharisees and Herodians," two groups with deep, though different, concerns about the occupation. Their question concerning taxes ("Is it lawful to pay taxes to Caesar, or not?" RSV) is not innocent but a veiled, opaque public test. When Jesus inspects a coin, sees Caesar's image, and directs them to "render to Caesar the things that are Caesar's," we can fairly interpret this as a refusal to support the tax revolt. Some scholars see this revolt as the beginning of the Zealot movement (*Antiquities*, 18.1) and this passage as Jesus' explicit denial of their agenda. The kingdom he advocated could not be co-opted by a nationalistic movement that sought to win back the land by force.[4]

Matthew records an even more direct test. In Matthew 17.24–27 tax collectors ask Jesus' disciples if he "pays the tax." In this case it is the annual Temple tax – an entirely different matter from the tax revolt against Rome. Nevertheless the half-shekel tax was controversial and denied by some (including Qumran) as an invention of the Pharisees.

Jesus acknowledges that such taxes are the prerogative of kings who place these burdens particularly on those who are not their sons. Jesus suggests that sons (of kings) do not pay such taxes but he will pay so as not to bring offense. Jesus then performs a miracle where Simon Peter finds a coin in a fish's mouth and pays up. Once again Jesus does what is required, conforming to those "kings" who would levy taxes. Cooperation is chosen above resistance; compliance is endorsed over refusal.

Continuity and discontinuity

Aside from the explicit question of resistance, there are signs in Jesus' ministry where he shows genuine continuity with the Jews' strong identity with the land.[5] His life begins and ends within the ancient inheritance treasured in Judaism's Scriptures. His birth in Bethlehem evokes memories not only of David and his history there (1 Samuel 17) but the many Old Testament references to the historic Judean village south of Jerusalem. In the Hebrew Scriptures Bethlehem is mentioned 40 times. Jesus is also known as a Nazarene, from the city of Nazareth in southern (lower) Galilee, his childhood home, and while the Old Testament does not refer to this village – and it is also absent in Josephus and the Talmud – still, excavations suggest that an obscure village did exist in the city's current location with a population of perhaps 500–1,500. From here Jesus moved to Capernaum, a well-known fishing village on Galilee's north-west shore and a crossroads for much east–west traffic in the north. Excavations in the last 25 years have uncovered the remains of the first-century basalt walls of the community that lived at the site. And after Galilee, his life ended in Jerusalem, Israel's most sacred city. This has left many New Testament scholars with an interesting question: Did Jesus envision a mission to the Gentiles or did he see his work as permanently limited to Judaism?[6]

His public story began at the Jordan river – moved into the wilderness – and then began in earnest in Galilee. This movement beginning at the Jordan evoked memories of Israel's beginning with Joshua (the name "Jesus" stems from the Hebrew "Joshua"). Was this Israel begun anew? Was this a revived Jewish claim on the land? Jesus' continuation into the wilderness further provoked this parallel with Israel. His selection of *twelve* apostles pushed it yet further. Were these the newly imagined twelve tribes? In some manner Jesus was reliving Israelite history, restoring Israelite hope for a new life in the Land of Promise. And all of this would take place within Israel's ancient borders. From Capernaum, Jesus launched his public ministry in Galilee, and with very few exceptions, he worked within the *sacred geography* of Israel's Promised Land. Therefore we might say that Jesus' identity and outlook were formed in the land (not the Diaspora or land outside Israel); and he sought to realize his mission within the land (not within the empire).

Jesus' continuity with Israel's geographical consciousness can also be found in his command to the Twelve when they are sent out: "Go nowhere among [Greek: *in the way of*] the Gentiles, and enter no town of the Samaritans, but go rather to the lost sheep of the house of Israel" (Matt. 10.5–6; cf. Mark 6.7–11; Luke 9.1–5; 10.1–12). Therefore their efforts must be limited to the cultural perimeters of Judaism no doubt as it was located in the land. Jesus' instruction may be an order to remain in Galilee, avoiding the south (Samaria) and the perimeters of the region where concentrations of Gentiles would be found. Nevertheless it is clear that the full embrace of Gentile work beyond the boundaries of the land will not happen until following the resurrection (Matt. 28.19). This was a vision that was realized in the efforts of the early Church.

While Jesus lived his life fully respecting Israel's geographical location, there are also signals that he would not be limited to the national constraints that this entailed. In other words, there was also *discontinuity* with the Israelite commitment to the land. In Matthew non-Jewish magi welcome the Messiah (2.1–12), Galilee is "Galilee of *the Gentiles*" (4.15), Jesus is greeted and followed in Syria as well as the Decapolis (4.24f.), and he ministers on the east side of the Sea of Galilee, where the Gentile demoniac was healed (8.28–34, possibly from Gentile Gerasa or Gadara).[7] According to Mark, Jesus' feeding miracle (Mark 6.30–44) is duplicated on the lake's east side among Gentiles (Mark 8.1–10). Among the Jews (on the west side) he feeds 5,000; among the Gentiles of the Decapolis (on the east side) he feeds 4,000.

One striking aspect of Jesus' ministry is that he even locates it in Galilee at all. This region in the far north was considered *different* from Israel's Judean heartland. During the eighth century BC the Jewish population there had been deported by the Assyrians only to be replaced by foreigners who had been resettled themselves (2 Kings 15.29). During the Maccabean era (second century BC), the region was so Hellenized that the Jewish army in Judea sent 3,000 troops north to "purify" the land, kill thousands of Gentiles, and transfer the remaining Jews to the south "with great rejoicing" (1 Macc. 5.23). By the New Testament era, Hellenization only increased – witness new Greek cities in Ptolemais, Scythopolis, and Sepphoris – and this fueled suspicion about Jewish life there. These cities were mirrored by great Hellenistic cities further east: Gadara on the Yarmuk river, Pella facing Scythopolis, and Gerasa on the high eastern desert plateau. Every fisherman on the Sea of Galilee could see Hippos poised on a prominent shoreside eastern hill. As Matthew reminds us (citing Isaiah) this was a land of "darkness," a region in the "shadow of death," a place of Gentiles (Matt. 4.16–17). Why doesn't Jesus work from Jerusalem? Why not devote himself to Judea? Why launch his efforts from the questionable geographic margin?

One story in Luke illustrates well the tensions inherent in Jesus' willingness to consider favorably those outside Israel's geographic parameters. Jesus' inaugural presentation in the Nazareth synagogue began when he read messianic texts from Isaiah (Luke 4.16–30). And yet, the resistance of the town to his ministry led to a startling warning. In Elijah's day there was a famine and Elijah was sent exclusively to Zarephath, *a widow in the land of Sidon.* In Elisha's day when leprosy threatened Israel's life, Elisha was sent exclusively to Na'aman, *a man from Syria.* That day the reaction of the crowd was swift and sure: they attempted to kill Jesus not because of his claim to messianic status through Isaiah, but due to his seeming disregard for the exclusivity of Israelite privilege in their land.

We find therefore both surprise and reassurance in the conduct of Jesus' ministry as it regards the land. No record gives us an account of Jesus crossing the Mediterranean to enter Jewish communities in places like Alexandria, Egypt, or traveling north to Antioch, Syria. No record tells us that he entered Gentile enclaves within the land such as Caesarea-Maritima, Scythopolis, Sepphoris, Tiberius, Ptolemais, Gadara, or Hippos. (His arrival in Bethsaida and Caesarea-Philippi may be the sole exceptions.) He remains in Galilee rather than the Jewish heartland – yet he comes to Jerusalem respecting its festivals. He appears to respect the territorial limits to Jewish life in the land. And yet, having said that, Jesus was willing to step outside those limits in ways that both surprise and disturb his audiences.

This is also true of Jesus' central message: the kingdom of God. While he announces the kingdom's arrival within the land, in no manner is the kingdom linked to the territorial aspirations of Judaism – as were the "kingdom aspirations" of the Maccabean era. Jesus' kingdom cannot be nuanced into a political movement that might reflect Jewish nationalism. And yet the kingdom belongs first to the Jews. Similarly, Jesus shows utmost respect for Jerusalem – the city at the center of Jewish territorial commitment. And yet he can still call for its severe cleansing (Mark 11) and talk about its destruction stone by stone (Mark 13.2). The call from the popular territorial theologies was for the recovery of the Temple not its destruction. Jesus is at odds with the "land theologies" of his day.

Critical passages in the Gospels

But can we find explicit passages in the Gospels where Jesus and the Gospel writers exhibit an obvious consciousness of the land and an awareness of what the religious and political climate called for? For some scholars, the land itself has become a literary metaphor in the Gospels for how spiritual formation is perceived. James Resseguie has argued that for Luke, the desert, the inland sea (Galilee), and the mountains each symbolize some feature of connection with God. They are (respectively) a place of testing, a place without control (which God may control), and a place of refuge. And above all, the Jordan river is a boundary that separates the desert from the promised land itself.[8]

Seven passages deserve note.

Matthew 5.5

In the well-known Sermon on the Mount (Matthew 5—7), Jesus describes a radical inversion of religious values. Enemies should be loved; mourners comforted; and the persecuted vindicated. Luke distributes these themes elsewhere: losing life will save it (9.24); the first will be last (13.30); the humbled exalted (14.11). This reversal of religious priority is the key to understanding Matthew 5.5, "Blessed are the meek, for they will inherit the earth." Here Jesus is echoing Psalm 37.11 (which Matthew shapes using the Greek Old Testament,

LXX Psalm 36.11) where the land, inheritance, and the "meek" are placed in juxtaposition.[9]

Psalm 37 describes the reversal of fortunes that will accompany God's activity within Israel. Those who are wicked and angry represent the unrighteous who will share little of Israel's inheritance. They employ the sword and aggression in order to take what they think is theirs. And yet, God is not on their side. He will give the land to those who trust in him (37.3), who delight in his ways (37.4), remain patient (37.7), and are righteous (37.29). Those who are *meek* will be delighted when they gain the land (37.11) because they are the ones who least expect it, who have been defeated by the strong and the powerful. Psalm 37 describes those who are greedy and those who are generous (37.21); those who grasp after what they want and those who wait for God to supply it. The land will belong to the latter.

The Greek term *praus* (here *hoi praeis*) refers to those who are humble and unassuming and it is used both in Matthew 5.5 as well as in the Greek version of Psalm 37. And yet, as D. Hagner writes, "In view are not persons who are submissive, mild, unassertive, but those who are humble in the sense of being oppressed (hence, 'have been humbled')."[10] In Matthew's only other two uses of the adjective, this describes the ministry of Jesus himself (11.29; 21.5). 1 Peter 3.4 applies this to Christians. In later Christian literature it should be an attribute of Christian leaders (*Didache*, 15.1).

The gift such people receive is the land (Greek *gē*). This flexible word (used 250 times in the New Testament alone) can refer to the soil (Matt. 13.5), a region ("land of Judea," Matt. 2.6), the earth itself (Matt. 5.18, 35), or the inhabited world (Luke 21.35). It can also refer to the land of Israel (Luke 4.25). But since its use here in Matthew 5 springs from Psalm 37, Jesus' reference would have gained immediate notice among his listeners as a reference not to the entire *earth* but to the Land of Promise, the Holy Land. Moreover, Jesus refers to these recipients as *inheritors* of this land. This is yet another potent term for Jesus' audience. This word (*klēronomeo*, to inherit; *klēros*, inheritance) was commonly used to refer to the assignment of land in the Old Testament promises.[11] When "inheritance" is joined to "land" the allusion is unmistakable: this is the *land of inheritance*, the Land of Promise. "Blessed are the meek for they shall inherit the land."[12]

This leads to a scandal at the heart of Jesus' pronouncement.[13] In a world where the powerful were ready to make bold political and military claims on the land; where the strong assumed that they had the right, thanks to their position or privilege, to take what was theirs, Jesus appears as "the re-arranger of the Land."[14] Meekness leads to inheritance – the strident will walk away empty-handed. The great reversal keenly felt throughout Jesus' ministry – *the last will be first!* – has now been applied to the land, this land of inheritance, the land of Judah, no doubt the most precious commodity fought for in Jesus' day.

Does this mean that Jesus here offered a territorial promise to his followers? This is not likely. For as we shall see (and as commentators regularly show) while the land itself had a concrete application for most in Judaism, Jesus and his followers reinterpreted the promises that came to those in his kingdom. Their kingdom is in heaven (Matt. 5.3, 10), they shall see God (5.8), and their rewards will be counted in heaven (5.12). Still, Jesus exploited one of the most potent images of his day – the land – and refused to offer it to those who demanded to have it.

Luke 13.6–9

In this parable, Jesus describes a man who planted a fig tree in his vineyard. Yet when he came seeking fruit from it, there was none. The caretaker then proposes to the owner that since the tree has remained fruitless for three years, it should be cut down. The owner refuses but instead orders that the tree be given one more year of good care and fertilizer, and if it fails after another year, it should be removed.

For some scholars this parable was later historicized in the cursing of the fig tree found in Mark and Matthew (Mark 11.12–21; Matt. 21.18–22). While certain literary sharing may have occurred between the two narratives as they were formed in the tradition, many reject seeing the parable as source for the cursing because of their different emphases.[15] In Matthew and Mark, judgment on Israel is immediate and certain; Luke's parable urges forbearance.

The parable includes one vital line (here in italics): The caretaker argues, "For three years I have come looking for fruit on this fig tree, and still I find none. *Cut it down! Why should it be wasting the soil?*" The final phrase uses the Greek term *gē* which we met in Matthew 5.5.

It may refer to the soil (NRSV) or the ground (RSV); but it may refer to the land. Its use here is suggestive because it is linked to a potent symbol for Israel: a vineyard holding a fig tree. And if this link is maintained, an echo of passages in the Old Testament comes to mind where the land itself has an independent life in relation to Israel. The land can either spit out its residents (Lev. 18.28; 20.22) or withhold its goodness.[16]

Judgment on Israel for its lack of fruit may lead to its removal from the land. It may be cut away. This is a prophetic critique of Israel: the land cannot be possessed without reference to righteousness. Living in the land comes with preconditions of fruitfulness. The land therefore is not a place of security unless those within it maintain some relation to God. Marshall comments, "Is there a hint that another vine will be planted in its place?"[17] This idea of land that fails to be fruitful – used as a metaphor – was common in Judaism. The later apocryphal story of *Ahiqar* does this to a palm tree that lived along a river and tossed its fruit into the water. The owner is eager to cut it down but the dresser begs to save it (7.46). Such metaphors were commonplace in antiquity: lack of productivity leads to loss.[18]

Mark 11.12–14, 20–22 (Matthew 21.18–19)

While the well-known cursing of the fig tree does not refer to the land *per se*, nevertheless it evokes the same motifs embedded in Luke 13.6–9. Its setting strongly reinforces the parable: Mark "sandwiches" the story with three main elements: (a) the initial cursing (11.12–14); (b) the cleansing of the Temple (11.15–20); and (c) the final withering of the tree (11.20–22). This is an interpretative schema designed to tell us that the cursing is a prophetic act meant to symbolize what is taking place in the Temple: it is judged for its failure to produce the fruit of its purposes. "My house shall be called a house of prayer for all the nations...but you have made it a den of robbers."

This scene puts Jesus at odds with those who held confidence in the success of Israel's national ambitions for the land, its most important city (Jerusalem), and its Temple. These things were not sacrosanct, not above critique or criticism. Once again, residence in the land was contingent upon fruitfulness; righteousness, no doubt, and the Temple had been found wanting. Trees and nations planted in the land will wither (or in Luke 13, be cut down) should they fail to do what God desires. Being anchored in the land is no guarantee of security.

Mark 12.1–12 (Matthew 21.33–46; Luke 20.9–19)

Each of the synoptic Gospels records a major narrative parable at the close of Jesus' public ministry. And in some respects, it may rightly be viewed as the signature parable of Jesus' climactic relationship with Israel or Jerusalem. Extensive studies have probed the parable and discovered numerous debated ideas, and here we can only give a concise summary.[19]

Jesus describes a vineyard and its recalcitrant, difficult renters. The owner – now absent – had taken good care of the vineyard: it was walled, protected, watered, and pruned. His only request was that the tenants would pay him with some of the fruit that came from the vineyard. When the owner sends his servants to collect they are shunned and, in some cases, beaten or killed. Finally the owner sends his son, thinking that his stature would be persuasive. However, the tenants hatch a sinister plot: they decide to kill the son and thus leave the vineyard without an heir, hoping all along to gain the land in the owner's absence.

This parable is vital for our discussion since it is certainly Jesus' variation on Isaiah's well-known parable of the vineyard in Isaiah 5.1–7. The preparation and care of the vineyard is described (Isa. 5.1–2), its failure to produce good fruit outlined (5.3–4), and the judgment of the owner (God) proclaimed (5.5–6). Then Isaiah makes the parallel explicit: "For the vineyard of the LORD of hosts is the house of Israel and the people of Judah are his pleasant planting." The vineyard then is a potent metaphor for Israel *in the land*. And Israel's lack of "fruitfulness" is reflected in how it has lived in "the land" (5.8). The signature sin of these people is greed as they consume the land for their own interests.

The vine metaphor was not unique to Isaiah. As a symbol for Israel and its life in the land, it was used by Jeremiah (2.21; 8.13; 12.10), Ezekiel (7.6; 17.6; 19.10), and Hosea (10.1). The luxuriant vineyard is likewise a metaphor for the blessing of life in the land (Mic. 4.4; Zech. 3.10; 8.12). But most important, Israelites can be described as vines that have been transplanted out of Egypt and replanted in God's vineyard, the Land of Promise (Ps. 80.8, 14; Isa. 5.2). Ezekiel used the vine/vineyard image for the transplanting of Israel to Babylon in the exile (19.10–14).

These background images enrich the meaning of Jesus' parable in Mark 12. If the vineyard is the land (and its people), Jerusalem's refusal to accept the vineyard owner's son will lead to its judgment. Thus the parable ends with a surprising announcement: The owner will come and "destroy the tenants and *give the vineyard to others.*" Jesus adds, "therefore...the kingdom of God will be taken away from you and given to a people that produces the fruits of the kingdom" (21.43).

By speaking about the vineyard – which alludes directly to Isaiah's pregnant metaphor – Jesus is making a direct comment about the contingency of life in the land. Possession of the land is not a human prerogative. There is another owner – God – and the vineyard's tenants are accountable to him.

Matthew 19.28 (Luke 22.30)

Jewish eschatology looked forward not simply to a renewal of Israel's national life, but a renewal of its life *in the land*, a renewal that included a transformation of the land itself. Its crops would give enormous yields (Amos 9.3) and the land would be transformed (*1 Enoch* 62.1–16). Judgment would ensue on this day of renewal as every tribe on earth stood before God (*Pss. Solomon* 17.28).[20]

In Matthew 19.28 Jesus reassures Peter and his followers pointing to the promises of his kingdom which they will inherit. The Twelve will sit in judgment on the twelve tribes of Israel (just as in the Jewish eschatology) and this will occur "in the new world" (RSV). Literally, Jesus refers to "the regeneration" or "rebirth" (Greek: *palingenesia*). Greek-speaking Jews might use this term to describe the land following the Flood (e.g. Philo; Josephus, *Antiquities*, 11.3.96). Hence Jesus looks forward not simply to the dawning of God's eschatological rule from heaven, but to the land itself experiencing renewal and transformation just as in the Jewish expectation. Jesus' interest here in the land is in how it will undergo change and rebirth.

Matthew 25.14–30

For some scholars, this parable about risk, investment, and accounting may refer to the land. Here a wealthy man is departing for a journey and he entrusts various sums to his servants. Two of the servants use the money creatively and gain a profit. But a third buries it. When the master returns, the first two servants are commended, but the third is judged in no uncertain terms.

The instinct to bury money was completely understandable in the first century. In a world without secure public banking, burying money was often the best way to guarantee it would not be stolen. For this reason, it is not unusual for archaeologists to uncover "treasures" buried in floors, villa courtyards, even fields. Jesus is aware of the threat of money theft (Matt. 6.20) and even tells a story about finding treasure that has been buried (Matt. 13.44).

In the story the man buries his money in the "ground" (Greek: *gē*). This is the term we encountered in Matthew 5.5 which has a variety of meanings. In the parable, it could refer to the soil or the ground; but for some, it may refer to the land. If this is the case, it refers to the cautious, preservationist instinct in first-century Judaism to preserve the land in a world rapidly overwhelmed by pagan life. Rather than risk investments, the third servant hid his money *inside the land*.

Such an interpretation is far from certain since it requires an allegorizing of the story that is foreign and arbitrary to the story itself. This may be an innocent account of a man putting money in the ground.

Luke 12.13–21

Rabbis were known to arbitrate domestic conflicts in villages. And since Jesus is reputed to be a rabbi, he is approached by a man who is struggling with his brother over their inheritance. As we have seen, this term – inheritance – may well have an innocent connotation but it also was one more synonym for the land inherited by Israel. Thus in the parable of the vineyard (Mark 12), the tenants hope to kill the son and thereby gain "the inheritance," the land (the vineyard).

In the present story, Jesus refuses to arbitrate between the two brothers. Instead he takes advantage of the opportunity to talk about the foolishness of fighting for an inheritance which is temporal, which can be taken away in a moment by death. He tells the parable of the Foolish Barn Builder to underscore the point. After his estate is prosperous beyond measure, God visits him to say, "You fool! This very night your life is being demanded of you." The upshot of Jesus' instruction to the men is simple: this inheritance is not as important as the inheritance you have in heaven.

For those who were struggling to hold the land and fight for it at all costs, the parable is provocative. It is a warning not unlike Jesus' relocation of his kingdom: his will not be a kingdom that values struggle and conflict but will be anchored to heaven. And Jewish identity that struggles solely to hold the land may miss the more important place God holds for us with him.

Summary

We began by underscoring the dramatic and intense interest Judaism had in the land during the first century and argued that this atmosphere of political struggle must be assumed behind most of Jesus' teachings. Reference to the land – a subject of extreme contention – would have to be veiled and nuanced very carefully or else a public teacher would be drawn into the competing agendas of the activists of his day.

Jesus clearly respects the uniqueness of Israel's location in the land. He limits his ministry and that of his disciples to geographic Israel with very few exceptions. We have no record of Jesus working within the major Hellenistic regions of his world despite the fact that they surrounded and penetrated Galilee. For him, both Judea and its great city Jerusalem were sacred locales with unparalleled theological roles to play in history.

But this ushers in a surprise. Jesus is reticent with regard to debates about the land. He expresses no *overt* affirmation of first-century territorial theologies. He does not repeat Judaism's call to land ownership nor does he express criticism of the foreign occupation. He never elevates Jerusalem to such a degree that it becomes a focal point of Jewish nationalism. He even anchors his work in Galilee, a region looked upon with scorn by Judeans.

Jesus seems to follow a different tack. In his theological outlook, blessings do not simply accrue to those Jews living in the land. He points to Damascus and Sidon and the stories of Elijah and Elisha as models of *distributed blessing* for nations outside the land. But it is not simply foreign lands that might be blessed, it is *the poor and the landless*. Surprising reversal was a hallmark of Jesus' teaching. Those who are last will become first, those who are rich will become poor. Those who fight to possess the land will be trumped by the meek. In his most explicit saying about land and inheritance, Jesus says that *the meek will inherit the land.*

Walter Brueggemann describes this as a poignant scandal at the heart of Jesus' land theology. Those who possess the most and who have the most to lose by a revision of Jewish territorialism resist Jesus forcefully.[21] Jesus in this respect is the great "rearranger" of the land. And his opponents know it.

Brueggemann anchors in the Old Testament a theme he now locates in the Gospels. The land itself presented Israel with a devastating challenge to faith. One could *grasp with courage* or one could *wait in confidence* for the gift of land. One could seize the land or one could wait for land. The prophets consistently urged Israel to choose the latter. And here Jesus does the same.

Brueggemann finds moving symbols of these choices in the modern state of Israel. There is Masada and there is the Western Wall (formerly called the "Wailing Wall"). The first represents militarism, the second patient longing and prayer. As symbols they represent timeless choices that pertain to Israel in the first century, the Middle East today, indeed each of us. We may grasp or we may wait; we may seize those places we claim to be ours by divine (or racial or national) right, or we can suspend our desire in faith. Sufficient evidence in the Gospels makes clear that Jesus echoed the sentiment of the prophets that a messianic reversal was afoot, a reversal that Jesus' mother Mary once offered when she recalled the sentiments of Hannah (1 Sam. 2.1–10), who said,

> The LORD makes poor and makes rich;
> he brings low, he also exalts.
> He raises up the poor from the dust;
> he lifts the needy from the ash heap,
> to make them sit with princes
> and inherit a seat of honor.
> (1 Sam. 2.7–8)

In these verses we find a theological inversion which would bring land-loss to land graspers and land-receipt to those who bear promises but lack power.[22] Mary exclaimed at the birth of Jesus that in her family's loss and poverty and landlessness, she was witnessing something parallel:

He has shown strength with his arm;
he has scattered the proud in the thoughts of their hearts.
He has brought down the powerful from their thrones,
and lifted up the lowly;
he has filled the hungry with good things,
and sent the rich away empty.
He has helped his servant Israel,
in remembrance of his mercy,
according to the promise he made to our ancestors,
to Abraham and to his descendants for ever.

(Luke 1.51–55)

4

The Fourth Gospel and the land

The topic of land and holy space in John's Gospel is an excellent example of what C. H. Dodd once termed "the historical tradition in the Fourth Gospel."[1] A virtual renaissance in Johannine studies has denied the older view that this Gospel is the product of later Hellenizing interests in early Christianity, that John did not know the land, and that he did not truly care about its place in salvation history. Surely this Gospel is linked to the Jesus tradition and bears witness not simply to the later Church and its concerns, but to the circle of Jesus' immediate followers – if not Jesus himself.[2]

Nevertheless, this is a Gospel written to illumine or perhaps reinterpret the person of Jesus. John offers an unavoidable and explicit Christology. Episodes taken from Jesus' life are woven together to provide a rich theological tapestry. Thus imbedded in this Gospel are genuine reflexes that take us back to Jesus, his work, and the land – as well as theological reflections that probe new theological territory.

Land, geography, and theology

Land and geography in John are an excellent example of this phenomenon. Specific locations in and around Jerusalem were once viewed by commentators as purely symbolic. The five-porched pool of Beth-zatha (5.1–9) was once deemed a mere symbol of a failed Judaism until a two-basin, five-porch pool was uncovered by workers near St Anne's church on Jerusalem's Via Dolorosa (thorough excavations ran from 1957 to 1962).[3] John knows the pool and wants to relay a story about it. And yet the fact of the pool quietly slips from view as John moves to a new agenda focusing not on the man and the location, but on Jesus and his unique authority to work on the Sabbath and make himself "equal to God" (5.18). Current opinion is that the southern pool's steps and its water channel indicate a public *mikveh* (or purification bath). John has not missed this either. The subject of sin follows the man (5.14) even after his healing (5.8).

The same coordination of history, theology, and location is true with Jerusalem's pool of Siloam. In John 9, Jesus sends a blind man to wash here, and while John knows the existence and location of the site, still, this is of less importance to him than how the site can take on fresh meaning: Siloam means "sent" (5.7) and John even provides it for us in Greek in case we miss it. The blind man's healing is found indeed in the Siloam *mikveh*, but his true healer is Jesus, the "Sent One," who has come from God (3.17; 4.34; 5.23; etc.). Therefore Jesus becomes the new "Siloam." The traditional pool identified in the nineteenth century now has been overshadowed by the dramatic 2004 discovery of a massive structure nearby.[4] One stepped side of this pool alone is 50 meters long. And here as in Beth-zatha, all indications point to another massive public *mikveh* for Temple purification.

For John, the importance of location is how it serves to reveal the identity of Jesus. Places are not invented (as some have thought) but they are strategically employed so that we as readers can see what is happening beneath the surface of commonplace events. But again and again, John's knowledge of the land has been vindicated. Scholars have often been mystified by John's reference in 1.28 to "Bethany [or likely *Betharaba* or *Beth Ha-Arava*] across the Jordan," where John the Baptist worked (1.28). But in 1996 when the states of Israel and Jordan drafted a peace treaty and the heavily mined east side of the Jordan river opened up, the Jordanian Department of Antiquities located a large Byzantine complex and first-century pottery on the Wadi el-Kharrar, a tributary leading into the Jordan river directly across from Jericho. This matches our earliest pilgrim reports as well as the Madaba map – and anticipation for the site is high. John knows the land and only in recent years have we begun to respect his use of it.

Perhaps the most provocative geographical-theological move John makes can be found in his treatment of Galilee and Judea. As in the synoptics, Jesus bases his ministry in Galilee, and like them, John notes Capernaum as Jesus' Galilean base (2.11). But while the synoptics show Jesus coming to Jerusalem once (his final Passover), John records Jesus traveling south to Judea numerous times (1.29;

2.13; 5.1; 7.10; 11.7; 12.1). This routine of regular visits to Jerusalem is far more plausible, particularly since Jesus would no doubt attend annual festivals in the city.

However, in John's hands, this travel itinerary tells us more. In John's narrative Galilee becomes the locus of belief while Judea becomes the center of resistance. Judea exhibits marked cynicism (4.43; 5.43) and opposition (1.43; 4.1; 7.3; 18.15). Jesus' opening visit to Jerusalem (2.13—3.21) fails to win a following. It even comes with a warning (2.23—3.1): Jesus did not trust many of the people there despite their willingness to acknowledge his signs.

When Jesus finally decides to return to Galilee we hear again and again that the move north is a relief (4.43, 45, 46, 47, 54). In 4.44 Jesus remarks that a prophet has no honor in "the prophet's own country" – and then he is welcomed in Galilee (4.45). Even one of the first Galilean converts, Nathanael, is *"truly* an Israelite" (1.47). Clearly these narratives are making a judgment. There is a problem in Judea and, in particular, Jerusalem. The city at the center of Judaism's religious aspirations has now failed some test that will lead to its judgment – a theme parallel to many of the synoptic parables. Galilee, a place derided by those in the south (1.46; 7.41, 52), is unexpectedly the place of faith and hope and light.

The land therefore – Galilee, Judea, cities like Cana, Jerusalem's *mikva'ot* – exists as a means to another end. Without denying the realities of Jesus' historical life and ministry, John invites locations to evolve into iconic placeholders that bear more meaning than the characters in the story could know. Moreover, John's awareness of the land, its cities, and its symbolism tells us, as W. D. Davies once wrote, "the Fourth Gospel was in living dialogue with Judaism."[5] This is not a Gospel pursuing docetic ideas about God and revelation. This is a Gospel anchored in the historic realities of Judaism's first-century life in the Holy Land. A quick glance at the roll-call of places provided in the Gospel is astounding. And it shifted the thinking of many Johannine scholars who once viewed the Gospel with skepticism. Consider this catalogue from J. A. T. Robinson's *The Priority of John*:

> Some of the locations are also mentioned in the synoptics: Galilee, the Sea of Galilee, Bethsaida, Capernaum, Nazareth, Samaria, Judea, Bethany near Jerusalem, the Temple, the Temple Treasury, the house of the Last Supper, the court of the high priest, the Praetorium, Golgotha and Jesus' tomb. But a surprising number are peculiar to John: Cana, Tiberias,

Sychar, Joseph's field, Jacob's well, Mount Gerizim, Aenon near Salim, Bethany beyond Jordan, the house of Mary, Martha and Lazarus, the place of Jesus meeting with Martha, the tomb of Lazarus, Ephraim, the Pool of Bethesda, the Pool of Siloam, Solomon's Portico, the Wadi Kidron, the garden where Jesus was arrested, the door of the High Priest's court, the Pavement/Gabbatha, the garden where Jesus' tomb was located.[6]

This list is simply astonishing. And it makes clear that John is not only knowledgeable about the land but intentional in his interaction with it. Robinson concludes that this data reinforces "the conviction, borne out of the apparent authenticity of the topographical evidence, that the Johannine tradition does indeed reach back in space to the very heart of the earliest Christian community in Jerusalem and to the ministry of Jesus that brought it into existence."[7]

The land and messianic fulfillment

To understand the Johannine treatment of the land, however, one more theological motif must be explored. John views the incarnation not simply as a revelation of light to the world (1.9), although this is vital. John also views the incarnation as having a vital impact on the established religious systems of first-century Judaism. It is not as if Judaism is being denigrated or neglected. John is not anti-Semitic. This is not new wine that is too good for the old wineskins. This is new wine that so surpasses the old wine that one would never wish to go back. And yet, without the old wine the new wine would be incomprehensible.

This theological agenda is called John's messianic replacement (or fulfillment) motif. When Jesus arrives in Cana (2.1–10) the story typically operates at multiple levels: this is a simple Galilean wedding attended by his family, this is also Jesus' messianic introduction cast in a Jewish banquet, and this is foreshadowing of his coming cross ("My *hour* has not yet come"). The most critical image comes from the stone water jars themselves. This is not regular drinking water. These stone jars contained water used exclusively for purification washing. Jesus works his miracle on their contents: his wine transforms and replaces the ceremonial water on which Judaism depended. Tied to this replacement is generally the theme of abundance (an idea that is solidly anchored in Jewish eschatology). Not only does Jesus supply the wedding with wine, but he does so abundantly. After the guests have drunk freely, he provides the banquet with over 150 gallons of wine.

In the next episode, Jesus arrives in Jerusalem and makes his way to the Temple (2.13–22). Here again is an instrument of purification which Jesus challenges. Again multiple levels of meaning are at work: at one level Jesus is outraged at the business practices there. But other levels are also operating: Jesus echoes the voice of God coming to make claim on his Temple and we find foreshadowing of his own death ("Destroy this temple, and in three days I will raise it up."). But the critical comparison is similar to that at Cana: Jesus brings something that will replace the institution he confronts. Jesus speaks of "the temple of his body" (2.21) indicating that the stone Temple of Jerusalem will soon be obsolete once Christ has gone to the cross (see below).

The replacement motif threads its way through the Gospel as a major controlling idea in the so-called Book of Signs (John 1—12). One night Jesus meets Nicodemus, a ruler and teacher of Jerusalem, and soon we learn that Jesus is the great teacher and Nicodemus is left fumbling with answers to Jesus' questions (3.1–21). Jesus meets the woman of Samaria and we learn that the water of the sacred well of Jacob now will find replacement in Jesus' living water (4.1–30). In each episode, the old form of religious practice – often symbolized by water – is replaced by Jesus himself. He brings a new teaching (you must be "born of water *and the Spirit*") or a new and unexpected gift ("he would have given you *living water*").

Through chapters 5—10 Jesus appears in the midst of Jewish festivals and again repeats the replacement motif, exploiting some theme central to its history. One Sabbath he heals a man who is lame (5.1–18). But then we learn the real purpose of the episode. As God was permitted to work on the Sabbath, so too Jesus may work (5.17–18) and thereby identify himself with God. Sabbath therefore serves Jesus' self-revelation by providing one element that permits him to show his true identity.

On Passover he offers bread to crowds (6.1–14), but then a homily on Jewish manna leads to its deeper meaning. Jesus himself is "bread from heaven" (6.33–35). What Judaism sought in Passover (a commemoration of the Exodus and the great feeding miracle in the desert), Judaism can now find in Jesus, who will give himself in his death for the world (6.51). As Tabernacles examines the loss of water and light of late autumn, we suddenly learn that Jesus is now the water (7.37–38) and light (8.12) the festival seeks. Messianic replacement forms each narrative completely.

This theological pattern woven into the narrative of the Fourth Gospel is so consistent that it has led many scholars to conclude that John is not simply debating the merits of Judaism, but the Gospel is locked in a profound and bitter struggle with the synagogues surrounding his fledgling Christian community.[8] Essential items preserved and defended inside Judaism now have come center-stage in a theological debate between church and synagogue. And this confrontation is likely the best explanation for John's repeated polemical use of the title "the Jews," over 60 times. John understands Judaism and his community has engaged in a debate with it.

If John is entrenched in a debate with Judaism's treasured ideas and institutions – and if the subject of the land was everywhere present in first-century discussion (see Chapter 2) – it should not surprise us to see Jesus speaking to the issue of the land somewhere in his discourses. And as he does so, we should expect the same subtlety that appears at the various festival and ritual accounts.

Jesus and holy space

Is John willing to apply his replacement motif to Judaism's idea of holy space? In minor stories, this seems clear. The Jerusalem purification pools of Beth-Zatha (5.2) and Siloam (9.7) both now find their truer meaning in Jesus. Even the Samaritan Temple is not to be venerated but instead Jesus points beyond to truer spiritual worship (4.20–21).

The climax of Jesus' encounter with Nathanael provides an even more valuable case study (1.43–51). When Jesus and Nathanael finally meet, Jesus reveals to him things he could not have imagined. And then we read this: "You will see heaven opened and the angels of God ascending and descending upon the Son of Man" (1.51).

This is an allusion to the story of Jacob in Genesis 28.10–22. As he travels east from Beersheba to Haran, Jacob stops to sleep in central Canaan on a hilltop village called Luz north of Jerusalem. He sleeps using a stone for a pillow and soon a dream shows him a ladder set on the earth reaching to heaven with angels of God moving up and down. God's voice then interprets the dream and when he awakes, he exclaims, "Surely the Lord is in this place – and I did not know it!…How awesome is this place! This is none other than the house of God, and this is the gate of heaven" (28.16–17). Then Jacob names the place Bethel (Hebrew, *beth-el*, house of God), he erects an altar using his sleeping stone, and he dedicates himself to God's promises, saying that this stone "shall be God's house."

In John 1.51, Jesus is linked to this story.[9] If the location of Jacob's sleep was the locus of God's descent into the world – if this also came to be known as "God's House," then it is clear that Jesus subsumes these to himself. He is the "gateway to heaven" as well as "the house of God." So much is clear among most commentators.[10] But the *content* of the vision is often missed. The purpose of the dream to Jacob is to reaffirm God's promise of the land to him and his descendants. "The land on which you lie I will give to you and to your offspring" (28.13). And yet, if Jesus now replaces Jacob in the dream account of Genesis, Jesus is the new Bethel. Moreover, Jesus is now the recipient of the promise of Holy Land held by Jacob.

These two concepts, Jesus as the "house of God" and Jesus as the recipient of the land, now become two central themes in Johannine Christology.

Jesus and the Temple

If one were to speak of "holy space" in the Jewish world of the first century, interest would move directly to the Temple of Jerusalem. From a Jewish viewpoint, the Holy Land was the locus of God's interest in the world and Jerusalem was the center of the Holy Land. And within Jerusalem, the Temple was the focal point of most activity. These levels of theological priority were like concentric circles, ever closing on the one place of revelation: the Jerusalem Temple and its innermost sanctuaries.

It almost seems a misnomer to think of Jerusalem as a first-century city: it was a temple with a city wrapped around it. Thousands of Levites and priests served in rotation. During Jesus' day, about 18,000 men were working to quarry stone and rebuild a refurbished Temple planned by Herod to be the pride of Israel. The new Temple platform alone offered a form of colossal public architecture Israel had never seen. Some of its perimeter stones (or ashlars) weighed over 600 tons. The southern porch of Solomon was held up by 160 decorated columns each weighing 5 tons. In every respect, the structure was designed to impress even those temple builders of the Roman empire.

Mark notes the surprise of the Galileans when they see this place. "Look, Teacher, what large stones and what large buildings!" (Mark 13.1). John reminds us that its construction had been underway for 46 years (2.20). So it is no surprise that this building not only resonated with the national pride of the country, but it was a token of God's accessibility to his people. Here alone the one true God could be worshipped. Here alone sacrifice was acceptable. In its inner sanctuaries, God was known to dwell. This was "his house."

John makes a stunning assertion with regard to this Temple: Jesus has replaced it. Today among commentators it is a commonplace to say that Jesus replaces the Temple not only in John but in the other Gospels as well.[11] What John has already done with the historic institutions and festivals of Judaism, he now does here. Those features one might seek in the Temple may be found in Christ.

The first hint of this comes in John's Prologue (1.1–18). In 1.14 we learn that "the Word became flesh and *dwelt* among us" (RSV). This term for dwelling, *skēnoō*, evokes ideas central to Israel's wilderness experience. The Tabernacle of the wilderness was a *skēnē*, or tent, and God was known to "tabernacle" with his people (Exodus 26). Therefore Jesus is the new Tabernacle of God; what one hopes to find in the Tabernacle one should find in Christ. Moreover the glory of God, evident at the Tabernacle (Lev. 9.23) now is apparent in Christ ("And we have seen his glory," 1.14b) – as well as throughout his ministry (2.11; 8.54 etc.). This link between Jesus and the Tabernacle is strengthened when we see John's interest in the Festival of Tabernacles in chapters 7—9. Here Jesus supplies the principal images of the feast (water, light), supplanting them completely. Jesus is not only living water but the light of the world. Jesus is a new Tabernacle now living on the earth; a replacement for the Tabernacle remembered in ceremony.

This notion of replacement is reinforced when we read John's temple-cleansing story in 2.13–22. Jesus compares the Temple with his own body in a cryptic saying, "Destroy this temple, and in three days I will raise it up" (2.19).[12] And quickly this is clarified, "He was speaking of the temple of his body" (2.21). The instruction now becomes clear: the Temple/Tabernacle – that place of supreme holiness, Judaism's most sincere investment in holy space, now has been given to Christ. John's explanation of the incarnation is formed by the Jewish notion of holy space located in the great sanctuary of Israel. Jesus Christ now in his life represents the very thing God sought to accomplish in his Temple. But note the dire prediction: destruction of *Jerusalem's Temple* is also implied. As Jesus will die, so will the Temple. However, only one will be raised up again.

Throughout the balance of the Gospel, these ideas reemerge with surprising frequency. When Jesus arrives in Samaria, the woman deflects his moral probing by pointing to the sanctuaries of Samaria and Judea (Mount Gerizim and Jerusalem). Jesus then disqualifies both places saying instead that when the hour comes, worship must take place in Spirit and truth (4.23–24). In other words, Jerusalem's Temple worship is facing its own obsolescence thanks to the arrival of Christ. It is no surprise that the only other uses of "worship" in this Gospel refer to either Temple worship (12.20) or the blind man's worshipping Jesus (9.38). Worship should be directed toward God (9.31) and facilitated by the Temple. Jesus not only brings the reality of God into the world, but he is the *place*, the *holy place* where worship ought to take place.

The link between Jesus and the Temple also surfaces in ironic stories. In 11.45–54 the Jewish leaders are debating what they should do about Jesus in Jerusalem. They recognize that Jesus works signs and that the public follows him. However, they fear that if they do not stop Jesus, "the Romans will come and destroy both our *holy place* and our nation" (11.48). In this verse, "holy place" is an expanded translation of the Greek *topos* (place) and undoubtedly refers to the Temple. Then Caiaphas supplies this counsel: he argues that it is expedient for one man to die for the people rather than the whole nation perish (11.50). The symmetry is clear: the holy place and the nation – Jesus and the nation. Rather than permit the Temple to be destroyed, Jesus will be destroyed in its place. Jesus can stand in for the Temple.

If Jesus now embodies the realities of the Temple in his own life, scholars often suspect that John's narrative implies the departure of God from the Temple itself. In 8.59 when the Jewish leaders try to stone him, John reports, "Jesus hid himself and went out of the temple." This concept of Jesus' hiding or departing recurs more than once. The climax of Jesus' public confrontation with Judaism ends at 10.39 when they try to arrest him, Jesus departs to the far side of the Jordan river and remains there. The Book of Signs ends with Jesus moving away once again. "After Jesus had said this, he departed and hid from them" (12.36). The withdrawal of the divine light, leaving Jerusalem in darkness, is the final judgment of Jesus (3.19–21; 11.9–10; 12.46).

For many scholars this represents the final judgment on the Temple. Jesus is breaking with Judaism's "Holy Space."[13] The Temple was the center of divine presence in Judaism. Now, that capacity has shifted to Jesus, leaving the Temple empty. As Davies concludes, "In 8.59 we find the implication that for John, 'I AM' [or God] has departed the Temple, that 'holy space' is no longer the abode of the Divine Presence. The Shekinah is no longer there but is now found wherever Christ is."[14]

If this Temple-Christology of John is correct, reflection on John's upper room discourses should follow the same theme. For a Gospel that regularly provides the place of events, oddly this scene provides no location. *Divine space is now no longer located in a place but in a person.* The disciples are cleansed by ritual washing just as worshippers were cleansed at the Temple *mikva'ot* (13.1–20). They are readied to "see the Father" (14.8–11) and to learn about the true nature of "my Father's house" (14.2). The last time Jesus used this phrase was in Jerusalem at the Temple (2.16). However, the disciples are directed away from Jerusalem's Temple to the many rooms found in God's house. These "rooms" are in reality found not within the walls of an earthly temple, but instead will be found when Christ indwells each believer (14.23). As the Temple is holy, so now, Christ's indwelling will bring to his disciples a holiness that is no different (17.17–19; cf. 1 Cor. 16.19).[15]

John understands the deep Jewish commitment to holy space. And the Temple was the premier example of this. However, this is where John's own Christology enters the picture. In Christ, the Temple had been eclipsed. In Christ, the holiest of all Judaism's places had found their fulfillment.

Jesus and the vineyard

Most interpretations of the vine homily in John 15 see a primary connection with the Christian Eucharist.[16] To be sure, the search to unravel the meaning of the vine metaphor has been exhaustive, combing Gnostic, Mandean, Old Testament, and Jewish sources.[17] Even when commentators acknowledge the substantial Old Testament vineyard parallels (Isa. 5.1–7; 27.2–6; Ps. 80.9; Ezek. 17; etc.), still, because the parallels are not exact, they deduce that the eucharistic setting has been formative.

But perhaps the more important question is not about the precision of parallels, but the *cultural weight* of the metaphor itself and how it served the communities who used it. The vine – regardless of its metaphorical application – was widely used in a variety of ways throughout Hebrew literature. Thus it seems appropriate for us to question the exclusivity of the eucharistic interpretation. The vine had a far more diverse and popular usage particularly in agrarian societies like Israel. In addition to representing the land, Judaism used it metaphorically both for wisdom (Ecclus. 24.27) and the Messiah (*2 Baruch* 39.7). A golden vine even served as a prominent decoration on the gates of Herod's Temple to represent the flourishing of Israel in the land (Josephus, *Wars*, 5.210). Even the early Christians, who were no strangers to the eucharistic setting, could use the vine as a symbol for other things *in their Eucharist liturgies* (*Didache*, 9.2).

Interpreters of John 15 may be strongly influenced by what they bring to the text by way of presupposition about the early Church's worship and how its experience formed the content of the Gospels. But it may be that an earlier, more basic concern now foreign to us was at the center of Jesus' thinking. It was a concern about the land and place and sacred space so central to the Jewish consciousness.

John 15.1–6 is the Fourth Gospel's most profound theological relocation of Israel's "holy space." This suggestion, offered once by A. Jaubert, has generally been overlooked by writers.[18] The central interpretative reference point is Israel's belief that the land itself is a source of life and hope and future. And a principal metaphor describing this rootedness in the land is the vineyard. The vineyard and the grapevine both in antiquity and today have supplied Middle Eastern culture with abundant pictures of life.[19] Thus Psalm 80.7–13 describes Israel as a vine transplanted from Egypt to Canaan and Canaan then becomes God's vineyard.

> Restore us, O God of hosts; let your face shine, that we may
>   be saved.
> You brought a vine out of Egypt; you drove out the nations
>   and planted it.

> You cleared the ground for it; it took deep root and filled
> the land.
> The mountains were covered with its shade, the mighty cedars
> with its branches;
> it sent out its branches to the sea, and its shoots to the River.
> Why then have you broken down its walls, so that all who pass
> along the way pluck its fruit?
> The boar from the forest ravages it, and all that move in the
> field feed on it.
> Turn again, O God of hosts; look down from heaven, and see;
> have regard for this vine, the stock that your right hand
> planted.

Hosea 10.1 makes the analogy explicit: "Israel is a luxuriant vine that yields its fruit." The Old Testament prophets Jeremiah (2.21; 5.10; 12.11f.), Ezekiel (15.1–8; 17.1–10; 19.10–14), and Isaiah (27.2–6) all make ample use of this imagery as do Sirach (24.27) and *2 Baruch* (39.7). Occasionally the metaphor becomes elastic making Israel not simply a vine, but the vineyard itself in the land. This is seen in Isaiah's well-known song of the vineyard in chapter 5: "For the vineyard of the LORD of Hosts is the House of Israel" (5.7). Thus the primary Old Testament metaphor depicts the land as a vineyard cultivated by Yahweh. The people of Israel are the vines planted within this vineyard upon the land. Taken together the cultivated vineyard (filled with vines) is "the House of Israel" tended by Yahweh, Israel's vinedresser.

Similarly in the synoptic Gospels Jesus tells a parable making the land of Israel a vineyard which is visited by the vineyard owner (Mark 12.1–11). Jesus' use of the vineyard as metaphor for the land shows that he has adopted this common usage well-known in Judaism. And yet here Jesus changes the terms of the metaphor. The people of Israel are not vines in the vineyard but tenants. The vines, therefore, are a part of the vineyard itself. The vines carry the symbolic value of Israel-as-land, vines and vineyard working closely together to make a composite image.

The crux for John 15 is that Jesus is changing the place of rootedness for Israel. The commonplace prophetic metaphor (the land as vineyard, the people of Israel as vines) now undergoes a dramatic shift. God's vineyard, the land of Israel, now has only one vine: Jesus. The people of Israel cannot claim to be planted as vines in the land;

they cannot be *rooted* in the vineyard unless first they are *grafted* into Jesus. Other vines are not true (15.1). Branches that attempt living in the land, the vineyard, which refuse to be attached to Jesus will be cast out (15.6). In John 15 we are given a completely new metaphor: God the vinedresser now has one vine growing in his vineyard. And the only means of attachment to the land is through this one vine, Jesus Christ.

This Christological emphasis is simply the Johannine replacement motif at work once more. Now in John 15 we learn that Jesus is the vine, a potent metaphor for Israel itself. He offers what attachment to the land once promised: rootedness and hope and life. As the final "I AM" saying, John 15.1 therefore is the culmination of the images paraded throughout the Gospel showing that Jesus replaces what is at the heart of Jewish faith. The Fourth Gospel is transferring spatial, earthbound gifts from God and connecting them to a living person, Jesus Christ.

God the Father is now cultivating a vineyard in which only one life-giving vine grows. Attachment to this vine and this vine alone gives the benefits of life once promised through the land. And as Isaiah and the other prophets pressed the vine metaphor to show Israel's lack of good fruit, Jesus promises that fruit-bearing will be natural to all those growing in him (15.2–5).

The family of concepts that draws together John 15 and the land centers on Israel's quest for life and fruitfulness under the watchful eye of God. John's Christology urges that this quest will not be satisfied with religious territory, with the real estate of Judea, Samaria, or Galilee, any more than it will be satisfied with religious ritual. In the messianic age, God's vineyard has one vine, Christ, and all must be grafted into him. Those who pursue territory, religious turf, motivated by the expectation that it is theirs by privilege hoping that God will bless their endeavor, are sorely mistaken. Johannine Christology could not be clearer. Only one person, Jesus, is the way to such nearness to God. He alone is attached to God's vineyard. He alone is the way to God's Holy Space, to God's Holy Land. "The way" is not territorial. It is spiritual. It is to be in the Father's presence (John 14.1–11). Just as the Samaritan woman of John 4 learned that Jerusalem was no longer *a place* of true worship (and that worship in Spirit is what the Father seeks), so now the land as *holy place* cannot be an avenue to the blessings of God.

Therefore John 15 is in fact a careful critique of the territorial religion of Judaism. The prophets of the Old Testament employed the vine metaphor to urge Israel to greater righteousness – to cultivate the vineyard. In some cases they used the metaphor to encourage Israel, saying that the land itself was God's vineyard and his gift to the people. In a way reminiscent of Diaspora Judaism, Jesus points away from the vineyard as place, as a territory of hills and valleys, cisterns and streams. In a word, *Jesus spiritualizes the land.*

But if we are to be grafted into Jesus, we might ask the next logical question: What has happened to the vineyard? Is Jesus then rooted in the vineyard, the land of Israel? Is Jesus the means of gaining the land? On the contrary, Jesus is *rooted* in the Father; he is one with the Father (John 17.11). The Johannine replacement motif characteristically exploits those elements which the Jewish ritual offers and then ignores any further application of the symbols found there. Jesus similarly empties Tabernacles of its ritual significance and then leaves the ceremony behind, offering the light and water once offered there. In John 15, Jesus exploits the vineyard metaphor in order to take from it what Judaism had sought from the land. Now Jesus is the sole source of life and hope and future. The land as holy territory therefore should now recede from the concerns of God's people. The vineyard is no longer an object of religious desire as it once had been.

Summary

John's theological portrait of Jesus and the land echoes and develops themes heard in the synoptic Gospels. In those Gospels, Jesus' disregard for the territorial interests of his generation stands out. He does not value Jewish nationalism tied to divine claims for the land. He does not engage in consultations that might secure the land from the Roman occupation. He is even willing to bless the occupier and hold up models such as Elijah and Elisha who traveled the land to bless residents in Damascus and Sidon. And when he does refer to the land, he does not encourage those who aspire to take it – the powerful, the "landed," the rich. He offers it instead to the poor, the powerless, the "landless." *Blessed are the meek.* In the synoptic Gospels, the land is enveloped into Jesus' theology of reversal. Those with power and privilege do not gain what they wish. Those with empty hands now gain full measure.

In the Fourth Gospel, the land is subsumed within John's theology of Christological replacement/fulfillment. Christ is the new avenue to God, the unexpected nexus between the Father and his people, the exclusive place of revelation and glory. What Judaism sought in its festivals and institutions, it can now find in Christ. What it sought in its Temple is now fulfilled in Christ. And the energies Judaism directed to the land must now be redirected to the One Vine of the vineyard who encompassed in his life the very promises life in the land had to offer.

The earliest readers/hearers of John's Gospel would have been surprised to meet Christians who claimed a territorial theology. They would have been surprised to think that Christians still believed they could find in the land blessing or promise or life apart from the divine life located in Jesus. This instinct so deeply anchored in Johannine spirituality perhaps explains how this community (made up of Jews and Gentiles) was content to remain living in Ephesus – if the later traditions are correct. They felt no need to live in the land. And this view – that every land might now have a divine claim on it – soon became the hallmark of Christian life and mission in the earliest days. Not surprisingly, Christians refused to fight for the land in the great war of AD 66–70. They fled, according to Eusebius, to the great Decapolis city of Pella on the east side of the Jordan river ("The people belonging to the church at Jerusalem had been ordered…to leave the city and dwell in a town of Peraea called Pella." *Ecclesiastical History*, 3.5). Nor did Christians fight for the land in the Bar Kokhba rebellion of AD 132–5. The vineyard they loved was centered on Jesus and his life and this could be gained in any country.

5

The book of Acts and the land

A cursory reading of early Christian history immediately recalls the context of Diaspora Judaism (see Chapter 2). Luke is a committed Hellenist who is close friends with many Diaspora Jewish Christians. And even if his history of early Christianity is shaped by his theological or cultural interests, still, Luke is painting an ideal picture that likely represents the views of many in the early Church.

If we follow his account, early Christianity is born at Pentecost and immediately converts a roll-call of Diaspora Jews who are in Jerusalem (Acts 2.9–11). From the east: Parthians, Medes, Elamites (Persians), Mesopotamians, and Arabs. From the west: pilgrims from Cappadocia, Pontus, Asia, Phrygia, Pamphylia, Rome, and Crete. From the south-west: Jews from Egypt and Cyrene in Libya. The main account of Luke's history moves away from Judea and introduces us to Paul, the quintessential Diaspora Jew. In the book of Acts, we follow him as he meets with synagogue gatherings throughout the Diaspora: Pisidian Antioch (13.14), Iconium (14.1), Ephesus (18.19, 26; 19.8), Philippi (16.13, 16), Thessalonica (17.1), Berea (17.10), Athens (17.17), and Corinth (18.4, 7). He knows churches in Diaspora cities and later writes letters to many of them: Colossae, Thessalonica, Ephesus, Corinth, Rome, Philippi, Crete, and Laodicea on the Lycus river. Acts has him traveling through Troas and Syrian Antioch more frequently than Jerusalem.

Even the lesser-celebrated letters of the New Testament such as 1 Peter reflect this Diaspora orientation. 1 Peter writes to "the exiles of the Dispersion" located in Pontus, Galatia, Cappadocia, Asia, and Bithynia – all cities in Asia Minor. Johannine scholarship similarly locates the Fourth Gospel and the three letters of John in a Diaspora cultural milieu (western Asia? Ephesus?) where Jewish-Christian life must contest with the philosophical temptations of the Greek world. Even the Apocalypse is addressed to churches exclusively located in western Asia Minor.

What may we draw from this? Early Christian mission did not see itself limited to the province of Judea that gave it its birth. The Christian community did not interpret its identity as linked to Judea or even to Galilee as Jesus had done. Indeed the witness has gone out from Jerusalem – in Jewish thinking, the center of the Jewish world – nevertheless, the recipients of the witness are welcome to remain where they are. Even if we question Luke's historical reconstruction as selective and theologically motivated, Luke's perspective provides a significant window into how an important Christian working with Christianity's leading spokesperson might think about the land. This is what many scholars of antiquity call a "geographical horizon" that determines how an ancient writer is constructing his or her world.[1]

For some scholars Luke is mimicking the geographical program of Joshua. As Israel entered Canaan, conquered it, and brought into being its own national life, so in Acts the Church enters not Canaan but *the world* making a similar claim on it on behalf of Christ's kingdom. This is a notion that we will see unfold in early Christian thinking: the unique claim God's people once had on Judea now extends to the entire world. Thus the promise to Abraham and his descendants is no longer for Canaan – but for the world (Rom. 4.13). Luke artfully plays this theme in his Gospel by underscoring how Galilee "of the Gentiles" is the center point of Jesus' work and identity. In the book of Acts, he continues widening the mission focus of the Church by contrasting Jerusalem with Rome: the new destiny of God's spiritual conquest.

At no point do the earliest Christians view the Holy Land as a locus of divine activity to which the people of the Roman empire must be drawn. They do not promote the Holy Land either for the Jew or for the Christian as a vital aspect of faith. No Diaspora Jew or pagan Roman is converted and then reminded of the importance of the Holy Land. The early Christians possessed no territorial theology. Early Christian preaching is utterly *uninterested* in a Jewish eschatology devoted to the restoration of the land. The kingdom of Christ began in Judea and is historically anchored there but it is not tethered to a political realization of that kingdom in the Holy Land. Echoing the message of the Gospels, the praxis of the Church betrays its theological commitments: Christians will find *in Christ* what Judaism had sought in the land.

59

Rethinking restoration

An amalgam of ideas converged in early Christianity's rethinking about what has been fulfilled in Christ. For the earliest Christians, a drama was unfolding and the land was one aspect – perhaps a secondary aspect – of the new reality now dawning in history. It was not simply the land that was undergoing a theological shift – it was Jerusalem and the Temple, two ideas that form concentric circles within the topic of the land in a Jewish worldview. If everything changed for the Temple and Jerusalem, it was inevitable that everything would change for the land.

The intriguing question posed by the apostles in Acts 1.6 – "Lord is this the time when you will restore the kingdom to Israel?" – unfurls a host of questions alive in the first century. Israel had sought its own restoration as a prerequisite for the day when all of the world would be subjected to its dominance and judged by God. This is precisely the sort of thinking that (according to Josephus) drove the rebels who took over Jerusalem in AD 66 (*War*, 6.312–315). It was thinking that surfaced even among Jesus' original despairing followers (Luke 24.19–27). "We had hoped that he was the one to redeem Israel."

A widespread Jewish view held that there would be an ingathering of Jews first as Israel was restored and refreshed as well as a later ingathering of Gentiles – many of whom would believe, be saved, and enjoy the blessings of God.[2] But this would take place in a restored Israel. So the question in 1.6 springs from this expectation: Would Jesus in his resurrected power now restore Israel to its proper place within God's unfolding drama? Would a political solution now usher in the new age of Christ's kingdom centered on Jerusalem? Would the land be returned to Jewish dominion along with the Holy City and its sacred Temple? Would God at last end Roman rule in the Holy Land?

However, what is clear is that Jesus does not envision a restoration of Israel *per se* but instead sees himself as embracing the drama of Jerusalem within his own life. As N. T. Wright remarks,

> Jesus' understanding of his own death and vindication must be seen in this light. He was drawing together the threads of Israel's destiny, and acting them out in pursuit of one of Israel's oldest goals and vocations, long forgotten in the dark years of foreign oppression: she was

to be a "light for the nations" (Isa. 42:6). God's house in Jerusalem was meant to be a "place of prayer for all nations" (Isa. 56:7; Mark 11:17); but God would now achieve this through the new temple, which was Jesus himself and his people.[3]

Jesus' correction of the apostles ("It is not for you to know the times or periods...") should not be taken to mean that Jesus acknowledges the old Jewish worldview and that its timing is now hidden from the apostles. Instead Jesus is acknowledging their incomprehension. He in effect says, "Yes I will restore Israel – but in a way you cannot imagine." The key is that they will receive power when the Holy Spirit enters them and they become witnesses to the world (Acts 1.8). In some manner, the initial restoration of Israel has already begun inasmuch as Christ, the new Temple, the new Israel, has been resurrected. The great theological shift in Jewish history had taken place already on Easter morning. Now the great witness to the Gentiles could begin. Now the new eschatological reality of God's drama would unfold in the Christian community. Peter Walker adds,

> Israel was being restored through the resurrection of its Messiah and the forthcoming gift of the Spirit. The way in which Israel would then exert its hegemony over the world would not be through its own political independence, but rather through the rule and authority of Israel's Messiah...Jesus' concern, now as before, was not for a political "kingdom of Israel," but rather for the "kingdom of God," (Acts 1:3).[4]

Or again, the solution to Judaism's woes was not to be found in socio-political remedies; it would be found in a new community formed by the Messiah and the eschatological Spirit.

Therefore the Land of Promise was the source of Christianity's legacy but no longer its goal. The political concerns of the land were a part of Christianity's history, but no longer formed its mission. The new mission would be the restoration of the world, not the restoration of Jerusalem and the land. The call to belief and obedience would thus pertain not simply to Jews but to "all the Gentiles" (Rom. 1.5) who now live within that field, that domain having God's claim upon it.

In a word, Luke wants to detach the promise of the gospel from the land without denying that the origin of that gospel is Jerusalem.[5] And he knows precisely what questions need to be provoked among his readers to make it clear. It is no accident that at Pentecost Peter's speech is heard by an array of Jews representing "the world." All languages, not simply Hebrew, now function on equal terms. The blessing of this new messianic era, according to the apostle, does not begin with a charge for these Diaspora Jews to come home to the land; the promise of the gospel is not found within the territory of Judea. It is a promise "for you, for your children, *and for all who are far away* – everyone whom the Lord our God calls" (Acts 2.39). As Walker describes it, the work of this messianic era is not centripetal but centrifugal: moving away from the center, Jerusalem, while remembering where it came from.

Stephen: a theology for the world

The link between early Christianity and Diaspora Judaism is explicit in Acts 6—7. The "Hellenists" described in 6.1 are Jewish Christians who speak Greek and are devoted to Hellenistic culture. Perhaps they are from the Diaspora. What we do know is that there is considerable tension between them and the "Judeans," namely Christians from the Aramaic-speaking community of Jerusalem. The church selects seven leaders each with Greek names (Stephen, Philip, Prochorus, Nicanor, Timon, Parmenas, and Nicolaus, a proselyte from Syrian Antioch). It is possible that Philip was one of the twelve apostles (Acts 1.13) who now has found a role and is counted among the "seven." But we cannot be sure. Among these leaders Stephen rises to leadership as a man of faith who represents the endowment of the Spirit characteristic of the community described in Acts 2. Acts 6.9 also tells us that there were "Diaspora" synagogues in Jerusalem at this time who welcomed Jews from Cyrene, Alexandria, Cilicia, and Asia. Stephen and his friends may have been converted from these.

The literary trigger for Stephen's speech is the accusations of "false witnesses" who claim to have heard Stephen blaspheme (6.11), and this leads to his arraignment before the Sanhedrin (6.12). The specific charges are leveled in 6.13–14, and for many scholars, they may hold more meaning than we see at first glance. "This fellow never stops speaking against this holy place and against the law. For we have heard him say that this Jesus of Nazareth will destroy this place and change the customs Moses handed down to us."

Stephen is accused of speaking against "this holy place." The phrase (especially in its use of "holy") could refer only to the Jerusalem Temple (1 Kings 7.50; Pss. 24.3; 28.2; 46.4; Isa. 63.18) and this is suggested by 7.48 where he denies that God lives in "houses made by human hands."[6] But it also might refer to the holy land itself (Deut. 1.31; 9.7). The Septuagint translates the Hebrew term *maqom* some 400 times with the Greek *topos* (place) – and this link is even more clear in post-Septuagint writings.[7] Of course, the chief term for the land in Hebrew is *'eretz* but even this term appears in parallel to *maqom* in places like Joshua 1.2f. *Maqom* can refer to designated lands, tribal territories, even sacred areas. Therefore Greek-speaking Jews may have thought of the "holy land" as a "holy place" where God himself is present, not dissimilar to the Temple. In the Greek text of 2 Maccabees 1.28, Stephen's phrase appears in a con-secration prayer, "Punish those who oppress and are insolent with pride; plant your people *in your holy place*, as Moses promised." Moses promised a holy land for his returning tribes – never a temple in Jerusalem.

This broader interpretation is reinforced when we see the content of Stephen's message about land and geography. The suspicion heard in court is pointing to Stephen's suspected disloyalty to the sacred commitments of Judaism. And while Diaspora Jews like Stephen would have sustained a personal respect for the Temple, it was in allegiance to the land where they demurred. Territorial theology failed to fire the imagination of the average Diaspora Jew.

The speech of Stephen (Acts 7.1–53) is not only a well-known interpretative puzzle but clearly one of the most important narratives in Luke's literary outline. The speech fits a pattern in Jewish writing where a summary or selective recitation of Israel's history sets the stage for some affirmation of God's mercy and covenant loyalty.[8] Psalms 105.12–43 and 106.6–42, Joshua 24.2–13, Nehemiah 9.7–31, and Judith 5.6–18 illustrate this type of recitation well. Generally such speeches will refer to the patriarchs, Egypt, then settlement in Canaan and its resulting kingdoms. The significance of Acts 7 is found in how Stephen uses his retelling of history to underscore his own unique emphases. What he omits as well as what he says are equally significant.

This is the last speech given in Jerusalem and the longest speech in Acts. And as it unfolds, Stephen receives such strong reactions that the speech leads to his death (7.54–60). As in the other speeches in Acts, a call to repentance and faith in Christ stand foremost in Stephen's message. However, another thread runs through his words that centers on the land. Stephen refers to "land" ten times in his speech. In 7.2–7 alone he uses it five times.

Stephen's speech is a study of divine location and divine revelation. In it, he provides a selective history of Israel concentrating on the possibility that God's voice can be heard and holy land be found outside the Land of Promise. Marcel Simon comments, "This may possibly reflect the mentality of a Diaspora Jew, who is eager to remind his Palestinian brethren that the history of Israel's divine vocation is by no means confined within the borders of the Holy Land."[9]

First, we meet Abraham of Mesopotamia who leaves the "land" of Chaldea to come to the "land" of Haran. Finally God leads him to the "land" of Canaan, the Land of Promise, but remarkably we learn that God gives him "no inheritance" there (7.5 RSV). His posterity will inherit this land, but we learn that they must first live in a land "belonging to others." The impression for the narrative is striking: "the land" might apply to a number of locales beyond the Land of Promise.

Next we meet Joseph in Egypt and are reminded how Jacob and all Israel made their way there. When Jacob, Joseph's father, dies, he is taken back to Canaan but is not placed in land that Israel owns. He is buried in the cave of a Canaanite. Here Stephen's speech reflects some confusion: Acts 7.16 has Jacob buried in Shechem in a cave purchased by Abraham from the sons of Hamor. Genesis 23 says that Jacob was buried in Hebron in a cave purchased by Abraham from Ephron the Hittite. Stephen's theological point is clear either way. Jacob is not buried in land that is his own despite God's promises. He is buried among foreigners.

Finally, Stephen introduces Moses, who gains the greatest attention (20 of 53 verses). He too has not been raised in the Holy Land but begins life in Egypt. After learning about his true identity, he becomes an exile in Midian, where he meets the God of Israel on Mount Sinai and there learns of his task to return to Egypt to free his people.

In each story important themes are sounded. God has not abandoned these lands beyond Judea. Although Abraham is in Mesopotamia,

God speaks to him there (7.3). Although Joseph is in Egypt, "God is with him" (7.9). Moses is born in Egypt and is "beautiful before God" (7.20). Midian and Sinai are outside the Land of Promise and still, God can speak there too (7.30) and perform miracles (7.35). Even when Israel travels through the remote deserts, God is with them and speaks at his tent (7.44). Most important, the ultimate revelation of God (his name) takes place at Mount Sinai far from Jerusalem. This new land in the desert of Sinai is called "holy land" (7.33) in stark contrast with the Land of Promise. It is as if Luke is showing us that holy land can exist outside the Holy Land itself.[10]

And when Stephen turns his full attention to Jerusalem in Judea, he reminds his audience that stone temples like that built by Solomon – and by implication like the one built by Herod and standing in Stephen's Jerusalem – cannot be the dwelling place of God. Clearly this is an indirect judgment on the centrality of Jerusalem and its Temple. Throughout the New Testament there is a distinction between things built "by human hands" and things "not built with hands." The stone temple of Jerusalem is among the former and cannot contain God (7.48). So in Mark 14.58 Jesus foresees the destruction of the Jerusalem Temple "made with hands" and he promises a new Temple "not made with hands." Similarly there is circumcision made "by human hands" (Eph. 2.11) and a spiritual circumcision "made without hands" (Col. 2.11). Likewise there is a resurrection body "not made with hands" (2 Cor. 5.1).

Stephen's point is simply that the human construction of a religious edifice is no guarantee of its divine operation. And to pursue a religion that fails to understand this distinction leads to tragedy and judgment (7.51). Such religion becomes fixed on what has been built rather than focused on what new thing God might be doing. And in this case, Stephen says, this fixity has resulted in many Jews missing their Messiah (7.52–53).

I refer to Stephen as a theologian for the world chiefly because he challenges the provincial nature of religious faith in Jerusalem. Shaped perhaps by his Hellenistic proclivities or, more precisely, by the culture of the Diaspora, Stephen outlines a theology that looks beyond the horizon of Jerusalem's native territorial outlook. Stephen's martyrdom should come as no surprise to those who understand the passion and anger that can fuel those who defend a territorial theology. Stephen has questioned the wedding of religion and land, or perhaps the synthesis of faith and nationalism. And it costs him his life.

Following Stephen's martyrdom it is not surprising that such thinking is pursued with zeal in Jerusalem (8.1). And it is equally unsurprising that another Hellenistic Jew – Philip – understood the implications of Stephen's speech, reclaimed Stephen's vision, and carried the gospel across an important cultural threshold: Samaria. The Samaritan mission of Acts 8 is no less than Philip completing what Stephen would have done given his beliefs about the land. And the continuing mission to Caesarea with Peter in Acts 10 is a necessary next step. The Church will cross any cultural or geographical threshold in order to realize Christ's claim on the world. This is the Church's mission.

Paul: a missionary for the world

It is telling that Paul is introduced by Luke during the stoning of Stephen (7.58). Perhaps Stephen is a forerunner for what Paul will become. Thus it would not be incorrect to describe Paul as Luke's premier example of the Diaspora Jew who now embraces Christ. His life in Tarsus of Cilicia, his skilled ability in Greek, his Roman citizenship, the ease of his travel throughout the empire, even hints of his Hellenistic education, together suggest that he is easily conversant with a Diaspora worldview.

On the other hand, we also discover in Paul a degree of psychological or cultural complexity that has inspired enormous analysis among scholars.[11] Paul is a man who lives in tension with Hellenism. His return to Jerusalem for study, his adept use of Jewish theology, his litany of credentials in Philippians 3, and his bilingual skills (Acts 22.2), suggest a thoroughgoing commitment to the conservative world of Judea and Jerusalem. In Galatians he describes himself as so zealous for the "traditions of my ancestors" that he advanced beyond most of his peers (Gal. 1.14). At his arrest in Acts 22 he quickly points to his zeal for these conservative values: "I am a Jew, born in Tarsus in Cilicia, but brought up in this city at the feet of Gamaliel, educated strictly according to our ancestral law, being zealous for God, just as all of you are today" (22.3). If there were Jews in Paul's Tarsus who were contemplating any compromise in the strictures of Jewish law and life, they would find an opponent in this Paul who had returned to the land.

Luke arranges Paul's narrative to underscore his intolerance for the early Christians who in his mind were Jews who had made a dreadful mistake to believe in Jesus: "I persecuted this Way" (Acts 22.4). "I...was trying to destroy it!" (Gal. 1.13), Paul can say. In particular Paul pursues Christian life in the eastern Diaspora (for example Damascus, and no doubt beyond). Paul may well have been a Sanhedrin agent bringing synagogue discipline to Diaspora Jews who in the judgment of Jerusalem's high council had deviated from essential teachings.

Paul's conversion provokes his stunning reversal: not simply in his new-found messianism, but in his understanding of locale. Ananias of Damascus provides the first hint of Paul's new mission: to come before Gentiles and kings as well as Israel (9.15). This Gentile mission is reviewed in the retelling of Paul's conversion in Acts 22 and 26, where one thing quickly becomes clear: this Diaspora Jew who returned to Jerusalem is now being sent back. Paul, who once took his orders from the Sanhedrin, now has taken fresh orders from the resurrected Christ. And these new orders have nothing to do with the preservation, protection, or renewal of life in Judea and its traditions. Following his conversion he immediately enters the eastern Diaspora and for three years explains himself among Jews in Syria and Arabia (Gal. 1.17).

The narrative of Paul's career in Acts follows his three missionary tours into the western Diaspora and his arrest and removal to Rome. In these stories Luke establishes in narration what he wants to convey theologically. Christian identity is not tied to the resumption of eschatological promises for Judea. Jerusalem still holds an important place in Paul's consciousness – witness his gift collection for the province during his third tour – and he returns to the city whenever he can. He even recognizes the importance of the apostolic leaders who reside there. But what is important about their authority is not where they reside but who they are in connection to the resurrected Jesus. For Paul apostolic authority is never localized in Jerusalem as the rabbinic schools or Jerusalem might be.

Paul's story demonstrates the geographic spread of Christianity and how it might find a home in any locale or any culture. However, in the speeches of Acts we find hints that this decision to reach beyond the Land of Promise has been considered carefully. Following Stephen's speech in Acts 7, the next major speech recorded by Luke is Paul's inaugural Christian sermon in Acts 13.16–41 at Pisidian Antioch. Paul begins with another recitation of Israel's history parallel in form to that in Acts 7. Paul anchors the good news of salvation in the election of Abraham (13.17) and in God's promises to him (13.26, 32–33). These promises have been fulfilled, Paul writes, in the resurrection of Jesus (13.33). He cannot deny that the defeat of the Canaanites led to the gift of Canaan for Israel (13.19). But this is not theologically anchored in the speech as it ought to be. The striking thing is that Paul here can refer to the promise of Abraham and *not* refer to the Land of Promise. This is what the promise to Abraham meant! But Paul is consistent with all the speeches in the book of Acts. Paul as well as Peter can consistently ignore the central elements in Abraham's life according to Jewish teaching: land and progeny. Abraham becomes a protagonist for the Christian faith, not the basis for Jewish identity in the land. Luke gives remarkable attention to Abraham in his writings (15 times in his Gospel; 7 times in Acts) and he might explain or paraphrase: The promises once given to Abraham have not been realized as Judaism expected: they are fulfilled in the life, death, and resurrection of Christ. And those who attach themselves to Christ – not the legacies of Judea – become his children.[12]

If Stephen introduces the earliest link between Diaspora Judaism and early Christianity, Paul becomes the public emissary to these communities throughout the Mediterranean. It is in this sense that I think of him as a "missionary for the world." There is nothing provincial about Paul, no hint of a territorial theology in any of his speeches in Acts, and explicit evidence that he believed the reality of life in Christ could be found in any land, not exclusively the Land of Promise. Paul does return to Judea on his third tour with a gift. And he takes with him a host of Gentiles. But this is an effort to strengthen the unity of the Church and not Paul's attempt to form territorial affections among Gentiles. In no instance does Paul direct his churches to demonstrate a loyalty to Judea *as Christians*. Territorial theology finds no basis in the apostle's thinking.

Syrian Antioch: a world-class city

Luke's formal introduction of Syrian Antioch appears in Acts 11.19–20 (cf. 6.5). Following the death of Stephen, persecuted Hellenistic (messianic) Jews who were a part of Stephen's community fled to distant cities. Some went to Phoenicia and Cyprus, others to Syrian Antioch. Two Diaspora converts, one from Cyprus and the other from Cyrene in north Africa, arrived in Antioch and there preached the gospel to Greeks. Christian leadership in Jerusalem had barely digested Peter's ministry in Caesarea when news came to them about Greeks who believed in Jesus and would be joining the Jewish believers in Antioch. The church in Jerusalem immediately dispatched Barnabas to lead the growing community.

In Luke's wider story, we must not underestimate the importance of the great city of Syrian Antioch (modern Antakya, Turkey). This is not simply any city – it had a reputation well established in antiquity. Begun around 300 BC, Antioch became the capital of the Seleucid empire and took its name from a series of its rulers. Its port on the Mediterranean, Seleucia Pieria (Acts 13.4), was 18 miles west and became the city's maritime gateway to the Greek and Roman worlds. When the Roman general Pompey conquered Asia Minor in 64 BC, Syrian Antioch became a free city and the capital of the Roman province of Syria. Soon its growth was exponential. Trade moving up the Euphrates from Mesopotamia or Persia could pass to Antioch, down to Seleucia and then out to the empire. The city was continually being enlarged and beautified by emperors. Even Herod the Great supplied its main street (or cardo) with columns. By Paul's day, only Alexandria and Rome were larger.

Luke records that the church grew in Antioch quickly (Acts 11.24). Barnabas was so amazed at its progress that he invited Paul (who was in nearby Cilicia) to join him (11.25) and together they led the church for one year. In Luke's mind, Antioch virtually rivals Jerusalem in importance. Not only does its church send out the first missionary team (13.1–3) but it continues to support Paul's travel efforts throughout his career. Whenever the apostle travels back to the east, he routes himself through Syrian Antioch, the base of his support (13.26; 18.22). On his first tour, he even bypasses Jerusalem on his return voyage.

In a word, Syrian Antioch became the base of Gentile Christianity in the first century. Its wealth, its access to trade routes and transportation, and above all its cosmopolitan worldview made it the ideal location for Paul's vision for the west. Perhaps it is this final value that sets Antioch apart in early Christian history. This was a church filled with Diaspora Jews and Gentiles for whom mission in the widest possible sense was natural. Allegiance to Judea undoubtedly played a role as the historic context of Jewish and Christian faith. But life there was not a prerequisite for faith. Moreover Antioch was willing to rival Jerusalem, challenging that church's leaders on matters of ethnic exclusivity (Acts 15.1–35). Even when delegates from Jerusalem including Peter arrived at Antioch and returned the challenge (Gal. 2.11–14), Paul could resist them, thanks to his enormous base of support.

In the narrative of Acts, Syrian Antioch provides Luke – and Christian history – with a "world-class church." It embraced true diversity, with Greeks and Jews sharing the same community. It was a church that found no prize in territorial exclusivity and would certainly see a territorial theology springing from Jewish faith as utterly foreign.

Summary

Diaspora Judaism and its culture is the plausible link that bridged the Galilean followers of Jesus to a world mission that broke the bonds of Judean territorialism. In order to cross this bridge the earliest disciples not only took their cues from Jesus' own reflexes regarding the land, but they were urged away from any territoriality by the Spirit who would empower their movement to new frontiers. The ministry of Jesus was no longer limited to Judea. Matthew's double warning, "Go nowhere among the Gentiles…but go rather to the lost sheep of the house of Israel" applies to his disciples (Matt. 10.6) as well as himself; "I was sent only to the lost sheep of the house of Israel" (Matt. 15.24). Anticipating his own vision of the wider mission of the Church, Luke has no corresponding saying in his Gospel. For Matthew and particularly for Luke, the resurrection sounded a new commitment to the nations (Matt. 28.19; Acts 1.8). God's work in Christ no longer experienced the gravitational pull of Judea or Jerusalem for its meaning or purpose.

It also seems clear that in the schema of Acts, the theological architect of this outlook was Stephen and his Hellenistic Jewish community of Christians. In Luke's mind, credit goes to Stephen for disconnecting Christian mission from Judean provincialism so that proclamation could take aim at the wide Diaspora world. And after him it is Paul who understood the implications of this new direction and implemented its application from his base in Syrian Antioch.

Of course, Luke himself built this narrative in Acts. He was a narrative theologian in his own right, a colleague of Paul, and a man invested in life outside Judea. Skeptical scholars will quickly point to Luke as the designer of Stephen's role and Paul's profile. But many others think this is unnecessary and unprofitable. Paul's letters alone show the deep investment in the Diaspora that was already underway when Luke formed his story, and Stephen's speech has elements in it that suggest Luke is using sources with their own pre-history.

Thoughtful Christians in the early Church – Luke, Stephen, Paul among them – were formed by the Diaspora and were reflecting on the extra-territorial dimensions of God's new work. This was a direct challenge, as Davies describes it, to the Jewish community "huddled" around the Temple in Jerusalem and the land. It was a challenge "to move forward, to cease to cling to the securities of the institutions of the past – the Temple, the Law."[13] Davies is echoing William Manson, who put it similarly, "Israel has been tempted to identify its salvation with historical and earthly securities and fixtures, and Stephen cannot but see some danger in the attitude of the 'Hebrew' brethren in the church."[14]

The early Christians under Paul's leadership – or a host of others that followed him – would have been astonished if they came upon men and women who promoted a Christian variation of Jewish territorialism. There is no evidence either within the Hellenistic mission of the Church or within the communities growing up around Judea that theological obligations required a political commitment to Jerusalem or the land. Thus there was no theological provincialism in early Christianity. The Church never forgot its heritage in Jerusalem or Judea and, as Paul's third tour demonstrates, the apostle wanted to keep fresh connections between Judea and the churches in the west. But there was no room for a view that elevated Judea's political interests above all others or that looked on Judea as bearing unique spiritual or theological importance. Remarkably even the location of Jesus' birth, ministry, death, and resurrection were not venerated until centuries later. The Church was forward-looking – Jesus had been raised and was elsewhere at God's right hand! His story was not a story about Judea and its renewal. It was a story about his resurrected life, his Spirit among his churches, and what he was up to in the Roman provinces of the Mediterranean world. Above all – as we shall see – it was a story about how God was reclaiming his entire creation, which meant the redemption not simply of the nation of Judea but the entire world.

6

Paul and the promises to Abraham

Reconstructing Paul's understanding of the land labors under a host of questions that have vexed Pauline scholarship for over 150 years. Was Paul truly formed by his Judaism? Was he the Hellenized genius who fashioned a Christian theology without reference to his ancestral faith (which he misunderstood or misrepresented)? Did he see God's covenant with the Jews having ongoing efficacy despite their unbelief? And what sources may be used to reconstruct his teaching since so many of his letters are regularly disputed?

It is impossible here to resolve these issues which others have addressed so fully in other places. Today, however, we can with confidence view Paul as promoting a theology richly integrated with Jewish themes, aware and responsive to the teachings of Jesus, and respectful of and invested in the Jewish world that denied Jesus' Messiahship. The certain Pauline corpus has grown far beyond the "assured four letters" of the nineteenth century and today its bulk is either from the pen of Paul or from some of his closest associates. Our treatment of the land in Paul need rely only on those letters that enjoy high confidence as Pauline.

Initial observations

There is little doubt that Paul would have understood the deep passions that flowed beneath Judea's national concerns for the land. We know a great deal about Paul's Jewish commitments: he was born into a Diaspora Jewish family in Tarsus of Cilicia and at some point arrived in Jerusalem to continue his education under the well-known Gamaliel. Here Paul excelled, embraced the party of the Pharisees, and considered himself well above his peers in his zeal for matters pertaining to the law (Gal. 1.14; Phil. 3.4–5). Paul believed that God's ongoing fidelity to Judaism had been realized through the remnant of Jewish believers in Christ located in the Church. On this basis he could add, "Has God rejected his people? By no means! I myself am an Israelite, a descendant of Abraham, a member of the tribe of Benjamin" (Rom. 11.1). When he defends himself to the sectarians at Corinth, he bristles at their charges, "Are they Hebrews? So am I. Are they Israelites? So am I. Are they descendants of Abraham? So am I" (2 Cor. 11.22). Paul viewed himself as a devoted Jew – sincerely committed to matters central to Jewish identity and life. In the first century it would have been impossible for such a man to be unaware of Jewish territorialism.

Peter Walker reminds us that despite some degree of ambivalence about Jerusalem, Paul's deference for the city remained firm, and this may lend some clue to Paul's view of the land.[1] He returned to the city regularly, he delivered the famine offering to the church there at some risk to himself (Rom. 15.25–28), and he respected the city's Temple. In Romans 9.4 Paul refers to Temple worship as one of Judaism's special privileges. And yet even with Jerusalem, Paul has reservations. He thinks, for example, of the city as a place in "slavery" (Gal. 4.25). Walker concludes that for Paul – and here we may have a vital clarifying insight into Paul's view of the land – Jerusalem and its Temple are places that enjoy historic respect but cannot claim a universal or lasting *theological* significance. Paul is pragmatic when he returns to Jerusalem, and his chief interest is in consulting with apostolic leaders there and unifying his Gentile mission with the church of Judea; but his writings betray another posture, a thoughtful and determined movement away from Judea as an important theological locale.

Davies points out a second observation.[2] Given Paul's Jewish commitments, it is striking how rarely Paul refers to the land or even Jewish nationalism in his writings. This begins with Paul's limited interest in geography. He never recalls the geographical particulars of Jesus' life nor does he refer to locations of importance when reciting the foundational events of the gospel (note 1 Cor. 15.3–8). Did he ever visit the Galilean villages so important to Jesus? Did Bethlehem interest him? Surely Paul knows that Jesus was crucified in Jerusalem, but he does not say so. The resurrection is of undeniable importance to him (Rom. 4.24–25; 6.4–9) and yet where it happened is less so. Paul refers to neither Galilee nor Judea. And the term "Israel" is used exclusively for the name of a people, never a place. Judea seems to be just one more location on the map: "so that from Jerusalem and

as far around as Illyricum I have fully proclaimed the gospel of Christ"
(Rom. 15.19).

In Romans Paul is eager to list the advantages enjoyed by Judaism.
In Romans 3.1–4, for example, Paul reminds his readers how the
Jews were entrusted with the word of God. In Romans 9.4–5 Paul
goes further, "They are Israelites, and to them belong the adoption,
the glory, the covenants, the giving of the law, the worship, and the
promises; to them belong the patriarchs, and from them, according
to the flesh, comes the Messiah." Among the privileges rehearsed
again and again in the Jewish world, the land stood out as one of the
premier promises of God given through the patriarchs. And yet here
Paul omits it. Of course, the land may be implied in his reference to
these "promises" but this is not explicit.

Third, we need to underscore the prominence of the Temple in Paul's
thinking. Among the three concentric circles of Jewish theological
geography (the Temple – Jerusalem – the land) the Temple stood out.
This was the ultimate place of holiness and revelation, the focal point
of Jewish affections. And yet Paul is willing to argue that the Christian
Church represents a new "Temple of God" (1 Cor. 3.16–17; 6.19;
2 Cor. 6.16). N. T. Wright comments:

> To Western Christians thinking anachronistically of the Temple as
> simply the Jewish equivalent of a cathedral, the image is simply one
> metaphor among many without much apparent significance. For a
> first-century Jew, however, the Temple had an enormous significance;
> as a result, when Paul uses such an image within twenty-five years
> of the crucifixion (with the actual Temple still standing), it is a striking
> index of the immense change that has taken place in his thought.[3]

The new identification of the Church as the Temple springs from
Paul's thinking about the new place where God will dwell. God
formerly dwelled in the Temple and now, thanks to the gift of the
Spirit, God dwells in his Church. Thus Paul can cite an Old Testament
text reserved for physical Israel and apply it to a Gentile church:
"I will live in them and walk with them" (2 Cor. 6.16). Remarkably,
Walker notes, Paul can apply this language reserved for physical
Israel to Christians *outside Judea* – Corinthians no less (Lev. 26.12;
Jer. 32.38; Ezek. 37.27).[4]

Clearly something is afoot in Paul's thinking. The historic devotion
reserved for Judea, Jerusalem, and even the Temple has undergone

change. What God has done in the Spirit and what has been realized in the Church has irretrievably altered Paul's understanding of a holy location, indeed holy land.

Abraham in early Judaism

The best avenue into Paul's thinking about the land is the apostle's treatment of Abraham.[5] The promise of the land begins with Abraham and is reiterated throughout the Old Testament as well as Jewish inter-testamental writings. God's promise to Abraham was not simply for a significant posterity, but for a land in which his descendants could build a nation. And this link between Abraham and the land is sustained in all the stories about Isaac and Jacob. Note 1 Chronicles 16.15–18,

> He [God] is mindful of his covenant for ever, of the word that he commanded, for a thousand generations, the covenant which he made with Abraham, his sworn promise to Isaac, which he confirmed as a statute to Jacob, as an everlasting covenant to Israel, saying, "To you I will give the land of Canaan, as your portion for an inheritance."
>
> (RSV)

The link to Abraham was also central to Jewish self-definition. To be Jewish was to be viewed as a child of Abraham, and this put one in a position to enjoy the promises extended to Abraham. In their polemical narratives, the Gospels make this view clear. When the Pharisees shore up their identity in an argument with John the Baptist, the prophet cries back, "And do not presume to say to yourselves, 'We have Abraham as our ancestor'; for I tell you, God is able from these stones to raise up children to Abraham" (Matt. 3.9). The polemic of John 8.21–59 turns on the same idea. Jesus' opponents attempt to secure their identity as true Jews by referring to Abraham, "We are descendants of Abraham" (8.33). And in response, Jesus invalidates their claim by questioning whether true descendants of Abraham would behave as they do (8.39–44). An echo of this connection to Abraham is borne out in the *Psalms of Solomon*, "For you have chosen the seed of Abraham rather than all the Gentiles" (9.17; cf. 18.4).

Abraham's potential link to Gentiles is fertile ground in Paul's thinking. In one sense Abraham is the pre-eminent Gentile. He was deemed righteous (Genesis 15) before he had received circumcision (Genesis 17), which logically separates his covenant righteousness from fulfillment of the law. Which is precisely Paul's agenda. Paul will make use of this theme regularly, since Abraham can now represent the prototype of Christian faith: one that may be attained by Jews who have the law and Gentiles who do not.

But Jews were reluctant to permit this full identification between Abraham and the converted Gentile. Judaism made Abraham the *exclusive* father of Jews, and in synagogue worship Gentile proselytes were required never to refer to him as "our father."[6] The great merits and promises that flowed from Abraham, particularly those that were tied to nation and place – territory – could not be shared with the Gentile convert. Jewish nationalism in the first century would not permit it. So while Abraham might serve as a model for the converted Gentile, still, Judaism showed no sign of universalizing the promises of Abraham to those who had inherited his faith and joined the Jewish world. Promises and benefits were viewed as derived through physical descent or ethnicity.

As Paul's Gentile mission grew, this is perhaps one of the apostle's earliest, fundamental complaints against his ancestral faith. If Abraham is the great ancestor of faith, if Abraham is the man in whom religious identity is secured, to exclude Gentiles from the promises that accrue to those who share this faith, indeed to exclude Gentiles from all that God promised to Abraham, was an unwarranted ethnic discrimination. One either shares the covenant blessings of God or one does not. Paul confronts this idea directly in Galatians and Romans.

Abraham in Galatians 3—4

The crisis that surrounds this early letter centers on the status of Galatian Gentiles who had expressed faith in Christ, received the Spirit, and been baptized. The inspiration for the controversy is teachers (often called "Judaizers") who argued that unless these new Christians embraced the laws of Judaism (represented in circumcision), they could not be saved and become a part of the Christian community (1.6–9; 3.1; 5.12; etc.). Paul sees this challenge as undercutting the essence of his gospel: the Judaizers may either be promoting a legalistic faith or they may be promoting their superiority thanks to the markers found in Judaism (e.g. circumcision). Either way, Paul takes marked exception to them and devises a careful theological strategy to defeat them. For Paul, the Gentile attachment to Abraham is sacrosanct. And if this can be defended, so can the Gentiles' place as heir to Abraham's promises. And if they are heir to Abraham's promises, they also become recipients of the premier promises of Abraham: nationhood and land.

A discussion of Paul's argument in Galatians immediately touches a broad array of theological issues. Even the nature of Paul's opponents in Galatia is uncertain: were they Jewish Christians promoting the law or were they perhaps helpful, concerned Jews living in Galatia itself?[7] Paul's discussion of the "law" today receives marked attention since it is linked to new perspectives that try to understand his relationship to Judaism. Many scholars believe that Paul has placed the mission to the Gentiles first in his thinking – not a complaint about the frustrations of life under the Jewish law. And therefore any idea that might impede that mission must be challenged, be it marks of Jewish identity (circumcision) or security (election).

Still other scholars such as Boyarin argue that Paul has been shaped by his Diaspora background and, because of this, has broken significantly with some of the historic positions of his ancestors.[8] This is the root of Paul's lack of interest in Judea, his use of Abraham for Gentile identity, and his neglect of Jewish privilege in both spiritual and political matters. Boyarin believes that "what drove Paul was a passionate desire for human unification, for the erasure of differences and hierarchies between human beings, and he saw the Christian event, as he had experienced it, as the vehicle for this transformation of humanity."[9]

Galatians 3.6–9

While some rabbis argued that Abraham knew the law before the law had been given (thus establishing his remarkable merit), Paul almost mimics this tactic by saying that Abraham possessed the faith of the gospel before the gospel had arrived. "Abraham believed God, and it was reckoned to him as righteousness" (3.6). Paul repeats this strategy in Romans 4.1–8. In these texts Paul cites almost perfectly the Septuagint of Genesis 15.6 (only spelling Abraham's name differently).

This discovery of righteousness apart from the law is crucial for Paul's thinking. Abraham is not simply an exemplar of faith, but he can now become the father of the Gentile. "People of faith" are thus the true descendants of Abraham (Gal. 3.7) and this specifically includes the Gentiles (3.8). The comparison here is not between "Abraham's faith" and the "faith [belonging to] Christ."[10] The parallel is between faith belonging to Abraham and faith belonging to Gentiles. Gentiles in Paul's view are participating in a faith once exhibited by Abraham.

This argument now becomes the basis of the truer meaning of Genesis 12.3, "In you [Abraham] shall all the nations be blessed" (Gal. 3.8–9 rsv). The blessings that accrue to the descendants of Abraham now come to those who share Abraham's faith. All nations who embrace faith in Christ can now participate.

Paul continues to reinforce this in the balance of the chapter. His opponents who promote a salvation anchored to the law have preached the inverse of the gospel. Paul even counterattacks: Those who preach such a gospel are under a curse (Gal. 3.10)! And of course this is the thrust of his debate with the Judaizers. But then in 3.14 Paul returns to Abraham and sounds the same theme by universalizing the benefits once held separate for Jews: The blessings and the promises of Abraham now may come fully to the Gentiles. Paul thus can champion a salvation that is "pan-ethnic" or perhaps "supra-national" and is no longer reserved in its fullest form for ethnic Jews.[11]

Galatians 3.16–18

Paul's most provocative move in this debate opens in 3.16. This is an inner-Jewish argument where the contenders are fighting to establish who can claim to be the true descendants of Abraham – or in ancient idiom, the true "seed" (Gk *sperma*) of Abraham. The full story of Abraham's blessed descendants is not fulfilled in a universalized gospel community of Jews and Gentiles. Not yet. That would be premature in Paul's presentation. The true end of this promise is found in Christ. Paul notes how Genesis repeats that the promise of God extends to Abraham and "his offspring" (Gen. 12.7; 13.15; 17.8; 22.18; 24.7). Then Paul notes carefully that the promise is never extended to many "offsprings" (seeds; Gk *spermasin*, plural) but to one "offspring" (seed; Gk *spermati*, singular) – and this one seed or descendant is Christ alone (Gal. 3.16). Hence the true heir to the promises that stem from Abraham is Jesus Christ. In Christ not only is the end of the law realized, but the beginning of the truest Abrahamic blessings is available.

There is no doubt that the Old Testament reference to seed is what we term a "collective singular" and Wright is likely right when he is willing to translate "seed" as "family."[12] That is, the promise to Abraham's "seed" refers to his many descendants (not simply Isaac) and this is represented by the singular (Gen. 13.15, 17 LXX; 15.18; 17.8; etc.). This reading is confirmed when we see that Aramaic translations (Targums) of the Genesis promises will often refer to "sons" in place of "seed." Rabbinic exegesis permitted such conventions – but also could exploit such turns of phrase to make theological points.[13] Thus the present ambiguous word ("seed") offered exegetical opportunities we might think odd. It could refer to one seed, Isaac, as well as to many. It might refer to one people, Judaism, while sidelining Gentiles.

Thus what Paul has done is entirely rabbinic and not eccentric. While there is no link connecting Abraham's seed with Messiah, the link between David's seed and Messiah was common. And this may have invited Paul's exegetical move.[14] Everyone knew that the recipients of Abraham's promise were many – as many as the stars of the sky. And yet Paul spotted a chance to exploit an opportunity that would narrow the promise to one recipient, Christ, and thereby reopen the question of what it means to belong to Abraham.

Two arguments flow from this: first, the law given by Moses centuries after Abraham cannot supersede this ancient pronouncement in Abraham's life. Covenants or wills cannot be annulled after they have been ratified (3.15, 17). The arrangement with Abraham is permanent and linked to the idea of a "promise" (3.18) never to the idea of "law." Second, those who wish to be attached to Abraham and his promises must now do so by faith alone. It is Christ who is the true heir; we can only become joint heirs inasmuch as we attach ourselves to him.

Immediately Paul has undercut the ability of his opponents to exclude the Gentile from the promises and blessings of Abraham – and he has taken up Abraham as the archetype of Christian faith, thus defeating those who would urge Gentile compliance to the law. And the apostle today would find himself at odds with many contemporary interpreters of Abraham in Genesis. For these modern "opponents" of Paul,[15] the permanence of Abraham's covenant in 3.15 means that the privileges of Judaism – the nation and the land in particular – cannot be undone. But this is the very opposite of Paul's intent. Only in Christ may the reality of Abraham's blessing be found for both the Jew and the Gentile. Jews may join this blessing when they embrace Christ by faith.

So with the words of N. T. Wright, Paul is asserting that God has "one family, not two." "Those who believe, those who are baptized into the Messiah, form a single family; they have come 'into the Messiah,' they have 'put on the Messiah,' they 'belong to the Messiah,' they are 'in the Messiah.' And this single family, redefined around and by the Messiah, is the single family God had promised to Abraham."[16] In a word, Paul has up-ended the traditional formulations and turned everything inside-out for the identity of God's people.

Galatians 3.23—4.7

If the rule found in Abraham – the rule of faith – is permanent, and if the realization of this faith has now been found in Christ, the custodianship of the law can be appreciated and set aside. The law was a custodian for sin; but in Christ the possibility of a new reality and life has been born through faith (3.22–23, 25). For Paul, this new reality found in Christ gives birth to a new community in which ethnic privilege no longer prevails. Nor do hierarchies of any sort: nation, social status, nor gender (3.28). Attachment to Christ by faith has leveled everyone's opportunity to have complete access to Abraham. "If you belong to Christ, then you are Abraham's offspring, heirs according to the promise" (3.29).

We dare not miss how this sort of argument sounded among Paul's Jewish-Christian opponents, much less the synagogues in which he spoke. Abraham was now being given to Gentiles who merely embraced Christ. And by implication, the inevitable promises of Abraham (including the land) were now slipping from the list of *exclusive* Jewish privileges.

But Paul is quick to say that his gospel is not simply centered on the elimination of Jewish privilege. Paul's gospel is not anti-Semitic because this new possibility of faith and attachment to Abraham through Christ brings benefits to everyone, Jew and Gentile alike. The arrival of new sonship makes all else seem like slavery (4.3, 8). And the coming of the messianic Spirit gives an ecstasy and privilege unsurpassed by anything the law could offer (4.6).

Galatians 4.21–31

If Paul's most provocative interpretative move appeared in Galatians 3.16, surely the Old Testament application that is most likely to give offense is recorded in Galatians 4.21f. Here Paul finds a parable in the life of Abraham.[17] Abraham's wife Sarah was unable to conceive. Therefore Abraham went to his slave Hagar and with her fathered a son named Ishmael. Later in fulfillment of God's promise, Sarah also conceived in her old age and gave birth to Isaac. Now for Paul these two sons represent two means of gaining what is desired. One means is by "flesh" (Hagar) and the other is by "promise" (Sarah). And for Paul these choices represent two covenants: law and promise (4.24). Moreover these two women represent two locations: Hagar recalls Mount Sinai and the law as well as present Jerusalem and its present slavery. Sarah represents a heavenly Jerusalem that is waiting to be revealed.

To be sure, Paul's Judaizing opponents in Galatians would have joined the Jewish community and taken strong exception here to Paul's story. Judaism saw itself descending from Abraham through Sarah to Isaac and Jacob, never Ishmael. And yet, here Paul attaches Judaism *without* Christ to Ishmael and bondage while claiming the lineage of Isaac for the community of Christ. Paul even attaches Mount Sinai, the source of the law itself, to this bondage. But Paul is simply continuing the argument he began in chapter 3. The true lineage from Abraham is a lineage of faith, realized in Sarah and Isaac and discovered now in Christ. Any who fail to share that faith are in bondage either to the law (4.5), or to the spirits of the universe (4.3, 9) – or even to an earthly Jerusalem (4.25) that is in bondage itself.

Throughout Galatians 3 and 4 Paul writes in the heat of polemic defending himself from opponents who not only question his authority to explain the gospel but question the essence of Paul's gospel itself. This is an intramural debate within the Jewish-Christian leadership about accurate markers of faith and benefits. And Paul has staked his claim. Contradicting his opponents as well as the Jewish teachers of his day, he has found in Abraham a true father for the Gentiles and he insists that those who truly share Abraham's faith will form a community of believers in which ethnicity can make no claim.

Galatians 6.16

Galatians 6.11–18 is the conclusion of this letter and 6.15–17 is a fitting summary followed by Paul's benediction (6.18). Here Paul reiterates that ceremonial religious markers such as circumcision, markers that indeed spring from the law, do not generate religious privilege. "Neither circumcision nor uncircumcision is anything; but a new creation is everything!" Paul is again leveling the field on which Jews and Gentiles stand: Faith in Christ leading to a transforming experience of the Spirit – this alone leads to the new creation typical of the sons and daughters of God. Traditional claims to religious privilege now dissipate before this new reality.

In 6.16 Paul then announces a blessing on those receiving this letter whose formulation has witnessed no end of controversy. The Greek text may be construed in two ways. (1) "To all those who follow this rule peace upon them; and mercy upon the Israel of God." The rule is no doubt the rule of faith that Paul has pressed throughout the letter. And in a translation such as this (cf. ESV) peace is pronounced on "them" (those who share the faith of Abraham) and mercy is extended to Israel (all Jews). Since Paul nowhere else refers to the Church as "Israel" this translation has strong merit. (2) Another view sees the final "and" as continuing the previous subject (an epexegetic use of "and"). Thus the NIV: "Peace and mercy to all who follow this rule, even to the Israel of God." In this case Israel and "those who follow" are the same. And here Israel is viewed as "other" than ethnic Jews.

The real problem is deciding the meaning of Israel. Is Paul offering a blessing on those Jews who do not embrace Christ? Or those who disagree with his gospel? These are unlikely. The "Israel of God" is an unusual phrase for Paul, and for most interpreters, Paul probably has in mind two ideas here: (a) those who agree with his teaching about freedom and (b) the new people of God in Christ which now includes both Jews and Gentiles.[18] This view is attractive because it carries the same conviction in Paul that we have seen through chapters 3 and 4. Paul's ecclesiology finds in the Church the true heirs to Abraham's faith and, hence, the true identity of Israel. Paul would never think that a Gentile church in some manner was *replacing* Israel. But he understood that in Christ the awaited messianic community had emerged – the true Israel, the Abrahamic Israel – and to this community the Gentiles could become a part by faith. This fulfills the expectation found everywhere in the letter.

But if this reading of 6.16 is correct, note what Paul has done. As earlier he had attached a Christian community of Jews and Gentiles to the heritage of Abraham, now Paul is willing to attach to that same community one of Judaism's most sacred titles for itself: Israel. Even the formulation of the blessing itself is markedly Jewish ("Peace be upon Israel"), with frequent uses.[19] This is perhaps the apostle's most stark example of universalizing the new identity of the people of God. The apostle is redrawing the definitions for self-identity. No longer based on ethnic or historic claims to race or identity, Israel now is the title for the people of God who belong to Abraham no matter their ethnic make-up. And with this redefinition comes a realignment of the privileges (the land?) that come with all identities.

Abraham in Romans 4

Many of the themes sounded already in Galatians now appear in what is Paul's most concentrated treatment of Abraham. Paul returns to Genesis 15, Psalm 32, and Genesis 17 in order to establish his argument for the priority of faith and grace in his understanding of salvation. And yet as a corollary of this argument – really an essential aspect of Paul's own understanding of the Church's mission – Paul uses these same texts to bring Gentiles into the fold of Abraham's children.

Romans 4.1–12

Here Paul anchors his understanding of Genesis 15.6 to an interpretative device employed with Psalm 32. To avoid viewing Abraham's "faith" as something God sees and rewards (thus making it a work of law), Paul employs a rabbinic method of exegesis whereby he links a principal verb in the sentence (to reckon; Gk *logizomai*) to another Old Testament passage using it as well, in this case Psalm 32.1 (LXX 31.1; see Rom. 4.7–8). What does Paul accomplish? Using the psalm, he confirms that God was not counting Abraham's faith as a good work, but was looking at his life as not having sin. Abraham believed – and this resulted in God's positive judgment or forgiveness. But since Abraham did not have the law and was uncircumcised, this reckoning took place *outside* the law. Righteousness was not based on a legal judgment of Abraham's behavior under the law; it was God's gift to a man of faith.

Thus God has not looked on Abraham's faith as a work deserving merit (4.4); but rather God offers to Abraham the status of "forgiven" *despite* his sin. Faith does not win this status. Faith recognizes or receives it. As a gesture of grace and generosity, God extends to Abraham a charity that was undeserved, and for Paul this is the template for the Christian gospel.

However, if Abraham was able to gain this righteousness without the law (since he was not yet circumcised), then Gentiles who exhibit parallel faith *without the law* are living in a manner reminiscent of Abraham. And as such they too may be considered people who enjoy the same blessings that Abraham enjoyed. However, Abraham was circumcised (4.10; Genesis 17). But this ritual gesture did not contribute to his righteousness but ratified it (4.11; Gen. 17.11). Therefore, Paul argues, Abraham can be the father of both Jews and Gentiles. "The purpose," he writes, "was to make him the ancestor of all who believe without being circumcised…and likewise the ancestor of the circumcised" (4.11–12). Thus Abraham belongs to both believing Jews and believing Gentiles.

Using Abraham's life, Paul has established a beachhead in his argument not simply for faith but for the impossibility that anyone would see the Gentile who has faith as having an inferior status to the Jewish Christian who bears the marks of the law. In this sense Paul has begun to universalize his theology, setting aside the privileges held among Jews (and Jewish Christians) who might see Gentiles as lacking essential elements of righteousness.

Romans 4.13–15

What Paul says next is striking. Romans 4.13 is the only place where the apostle refers explicitly to the promises for the land given to Abraham and in this case Paul fails to refer to Judea. Paul writes that the promise to Abraham indicates that the patriarch would inherit *the world* (Gk *kosmos*). The universalizing intent of Paul has now shifted from the Gentiles to the domain of Gentile life. In Genesis Abraham was to inherit the Holy Land. In Romans 4.13, his claim is on the world.

The Jewish claim on the whole world was not unknown to Paul. Israel's covenant vocation was understood to include salvation for the entire world, and this was based on popular interpretations of Genesis 12.3, "in you all the families of the earth shall be blessed."[20] Abraham is God's answer to a problem that emerges from Adam. A rabbinic commentary (or *midrash*) on Genesis expresses it clearly, "I will make Adam first and if he goes astray, I will send Abraham to sort it all out" (*Genesis Rabbah* 14.6).[21] Those who descend from Abraham (through Jacob) become agents of this solution. As Adam is to be fruitful (Gen. 1.28), so Abraham claims the same hope ("...I will make you fruitful", Gen. 17.2, 6, 8). As Adam claims supremacy over nature, so Abraham is promised dominion over Canaan.[22] Israel then is redeeming the vocation lost to Adam; Israel will recreate Eden and bring about hope for a restored life. The prophets reinforce this idea. For Isaiah and Micah, Jerusalem will be the city to which the Gentiles will come (Isa. 2.2–5; 42.6; Mic. 4.1–5). The rivers of Ezekiel flow from Zion and refresh the rest of the world (Ezekiel 40—47). For Zechariah the renewal of Jerusalem is the catalyst for the renewal of the world itself (14.8–19).

And yet Judaism believes that – and here we find Paul's departure from his rabbinic peers – given the many foreign occupations Judaism has experienced in the intertestamental period, Israel will also be the means by which God will restore divine order upon the world. Idolatry will cease and evil will be judged. And above all, this divine solution will be Judea-centric. In its most charitable form, Israel will be Isaiah's "light to the nations," providing guidance and blessing, calling the nations to worship the one true God at Jerusalem. And yet by some accounts, this idea of blessing the nations is strictly neglected among the rabbis.[23] In its most severe form such as that found in the *Psalms of Solomon*, Israel will judge the nations and in many cases destroy them (*Pss. Solomon* 17).

For Paul, Romans 4.13 is a unique return to Israel's highest calling for the world. Abraham and his children – defined by Paul as people of faith – now discover God's program not simply for Canaan or Judea, but for the world. The formula that linked Abraham to Jewish ethnic lineage and the right to possess the land has now been overturned in Christ. Paul's Christian theology links Abraham to children of faith, and to them belongs God's full domain, namely, the world. Wright compares the land to the law in Paul's thinking:

> The Land, like the Torah, was a temporary stage in the long purpose of the God of Abraham. It was not a bad thing done away with, but a good and necessary thing now fulfilled in Christ and the Spirit. It is as though, in fact, the Land were a great advance metaphor for the design of God that his people should eventually bring the whole world into submission to his healing reign. God's whole purpose now goes beyond Jerusalem and the Land to the whole world.[24]

This shift from promise to reality resides so deeply at the core of Paul's thinking that to miss it is to miss the true eschatological epoch that Paul understands to be at work in Christ. Robertson puts it this way: "The old-covenant form of redemption is indeed glorious and appeals to the human longing for a sure and settled land. Yet it cannot compare with the realities of new-covenant fulfillment."[25]

Romans 4.16–25

Paul reinforces his conviction about Gentile inclusion in the final section of the chapter. The promises to Abraham are "guaranteed to *all* his descendants" (4.16a) – to the Jew who keeps the law as well as the Gentiles who "share the faith of Abraham" (4.16b). Paul now interprets Genesis 17.5 underscoring the fuller meaning of God's promise that Abraham would be father of "many nations" (4.17, 18). These nations are now found among the Gentiles in whom faith can be located and where spiritual lineage to the patriarch is possible.

In these verses Paul is contradicting conventional Jewish teaching about ethnic exclusivity as it applied to the link to Abraham and God's promises to him. He is challenging the privileges claimed by those who hold Jewish markers of religious identity and denying them their advantages. But he does not see these points made about Abraham and Genesis as antiquarian. They are deeply relevant to his own era and every era where religious privileges backed by ethnicity are making their claims (4.23–25).

The traditional teaching that Jerusalem is the center of God's redemptive activity surrounded by many nations that come to her for blessing – this scenario now ends in Paul's eschatological worldview. Something of the new order has now been fulfilled in Christ. Traditional (and popular) Jewish eschatology must now come to an end. Gentiles are not on the periphery of the people of God; they are now in full communion with the people of God – their domain is God's domain, their land is holy land.

The paradox in Romans 9—11

Paul's defense of his own position with regard to Judaism and God's fidelity to his covenant people is set out in Romans 9—11. Here Paul continues the argument posed in Galatians 3—4 and Romans 4 that Gentile believers in Christ have joined with Jewish believers to form a renewed covenant people of God. However, what is striking here is that Paul now reflects on Judaism *outside of Christ*. This community of ethnic Jews which descends from Abraham and rejects its Messiah continues to have a place in God's eschatological plan for humanity. Judaism without Christ simply does not disappear. It holds its place. Given all that Paul has said about the need to rethink who God's people are in Christ, Paul here presents us with a paradox that some interpreters have found impossible to reconcile. Moreover, if the covenants of Judaism are still in force, are the privileges of those covenants still in play for Paul? Does this paradox extend to the land? Has Paul not already implied that God has revoked the territorial character of Judaism?

First, Paul affirms that God has not rejected Israel, because he himself is an Israelite and so are other Jewish Christians like him. Drawing on the Old Testament notion of a remnant, Paul argues that Christian believers are the new remnant in God's working: "So too at the present time there is a remnant, chosen by grace" (Rom. 11.5). Thus in 11.1 when Paul thinks about the question, "Has God rejected his people?" he replies emphatically, "By no means!" The key is in 11.2, "God has not rejected his people whom he foreknew." The remnant is the body of believers within Judaism who have kept faith with the covenant and God's purposes. And God knows who they are. Therefore the covenant fidelity of God may be discovered within the Church where believing messianic Jews are present. Jewish believers are now heir to the great covenant history of the Old Testament.

Is this remnant simply Jewish Christians? Not at all. In 9.25–26 Paul cites Hosea's reference to Gentiles: "And in the very place where it was said to them, 'You are not my people,' there they shall be called children of the living God." Where was this proclamation given? Jerusalem. God's holy city is the place where the Church – filled with Jews and Gentiles – as the remnant, the body of believers predicted by Hosea, will be announced fulfilling God's purposes.

Second, Paul develops the picture of an olive tree as an image of God's people in history. It has many branches and, thus, many people. Paul says that unbelieving Israel is like a branch broken off from the trunk of this tree. That is, unbelieving Israel has been rejected (11.15) and "broken off" (11.20) so that Gentile believers might be "grafted in" (11.17–19). "God's people" (the tree trunk) is a wider concept than just Israel alone. Unbelief and sinfulness have led to many being "broken off" throughout the years. But even though there have been these periods of judgment, God has never forsaken the "trunk," his people, in history.

Third, the basis of Israel's failure is at the center of Paul's understanding of righteousness. Paul's own religious merits were of no use to him (Phil. 3.4–9). His ancestral faith has the same problem. Merit with God cannot be found in something we can offer, something we conjure up out of our history or religion. God's righteousness works from our emptiness and thus is known to us as grace. If this is true, then Jews and Gentiles are equals (11.32), and Judaism cannot claim any historic privileges any more than Paul could. One cannot demand the promises of God – much less the land – based on religious privilege. Paul writes about his fellow Jews:

> I can testify that they have a zeal for God, but it is not enlightened. For, being ignorant of the righteousness that comes from God, and seeking to establish their own, they have not submitted to God's righteousness. For Christ is the end of the law so that there may be righteousness for everyone who believes.
>
> (Rom. 10.2–4)

Therefore in Paul's theology he sees the Jewish people *outside of Christ* living at a loss and under judgment (11.21–22). They are branches broken off. Unenlightened and misdirected. Belonging to a city in slavery (Gal. 4.25). Linked now to Hagar (not Sarah) and Mount Sinai rather than the heavenly Jerusalem (Gal. 4.24, 26). There is hope, however. These natural branches may be grafted back into place if they do not persist in their unbelief (Rom. 11.23–34). The Jewish people *outside Christ* may return to their location in the economy of God should they embrace Christ.[26]

But it is here that Paul opens his paradox, introducing a remarkable tension in what should have been a clear-cut theological conclusion. Pauline eschatology provides a place for Judaism without Christ. During the present time, Paul writes, Israel has become "hardened" (11.25), but in the future, after the Gentiles have been "grafted in," all Israel will be saved once more (11.26–27). Paul thus anticipates a future redemption in the plan of God that will include the Jewish people who originally rejected Christ. For the most part, Paul's hope for Israel is in future at the end of time.

But more must be said. If Judaism remains – even in its broken-ness – a people with a unique future, a people still to be redeemed and drawn into the messianic community, then it follows that they currently have a place of honor even in their unbelief. Note Paul's words in Romans 11.28–29: "As regards the gospel they are enemies of God for your sake; but as regards election they are beloved, for the sake of their ancestors; for the gifts and the calling of God are irrevocable."

Paul freely admits that Judaism now stands opposed to the gospel. Judaism without its Messiah is hostile to God's new purposes in Christ. Judaism has rejected the new covenant. Nevertheless, even in this disobedience, these broken branches still possess an incomparable place in history. Unbelieving Judaism is beloved, just as exiled Judaism was beloved in the Old Testament, and it holds an enduring role. For the sake of their history, for the sake of the promises made to their ancestors, God will retain a place for Jews in history. In their present condition of unbelief, they deserve honor. And when they accept Christ, be it now or in the future, their brokenness will be restored. Paul enjoys drawing out the metaphor of the olive tree to its limit. God is eager to see "these natural branches" grafted back in place. "For if you have been cut from what is by nature a wild olive tree and grafted, contrary to nature, into a cultivated olive tree, how much more will these natural branches be grafted back into their own olive tree" (Rom. 11.24).

So if unbelieving Israel is not rejected, if the gifts and the calling of God are irrevocable, what covenant benefits come to this Israel? Does Paul view the land – a benefit of Abraham's covenant – as remaining in place for Judaism? Is Jewish territoriality a part of Pauline eschatology?

Paul's bold treatment of the law, Jerusalem and even the Temple all point to an implicit rejection of Jewish territoriality. The former things of the former covenant – the Temple being our premier case study – now have undergone a permanent shift since the coming of Christ. And ethnic claims for the land based on lineage to Abraham now must be reexamined in the same way: Christ is the truest heir to Abraham and attachment to him – grafting in Romans 11 – is the one prerequisite for being a part of the saving purposes of God. Moreover God's promise to Abraham is not for Judea and its restoration but for the world. An ethnocentric territoriality anchored to ancestral theological claims cannot survive Paul's fresh rearrangement of God's saving purposes in Christ. To miss these implications is to miss the central theological upheaval Paul is offering to his readers as he rethinks what it means to be "God's people."

Paul and the Temple

While the primary avenue to understanding Paul's rethinking of theological locality is found in his treatment of Abraham in Romans and Galatians, still other important texts reinforce Paul's preference to universalize the promises of God away from the specificity and territoriality of his native Judaism. Paul's treatment of the Temple is an ancillary but vital detour for us. Three texts deserve attention.

In 1 Corinthians 3.16–17 Paul reminds the Corinthians that they are "God's Temple" and that the "Spirit of God" dwells within them. "For God's temple is holy and you are that temple." Here Paul is applying the sanctity of the Jerusalem Temple to the Church in order to give an ethical charge. But for him to do so we note how the place of the Temple has now been taken up by the Church itself. Paul does not explicitly say that the Jerusalem Temple is now obsolete or that the Church has replaced the Temple, although these ideas might be implied. Nevertheless there is a migration of categories in Paul's thinking: the privileged role of the Temple in Jerusalem is no longer inviolate. The Church has now assumed its identity.

Another glimpse at this theological migration appears in 2 Corinthians 6.14–18. In this case Paul is contrasting immoral conduct with a holy life comparable to the reality found in Jerusalem's Temple: in 6.16, the Greek pronoun is emphatic: "*We* are the temple of the living God." This is followed by a composite quotation from Leviticus 26.12, Ezekiel 37.27, Isaiah 52.11, and 2 Samuel 7.14. Here Paul is exploiting the language of Temple and priesthood to reinforce the moral obligations of Christ's people. They are to "come out" and touch "nothing unclean" (as priests). Paul even changes the wording of Leviticus 26.12 LXX. Rather than saying "I will set my tabernacle among you [Gk *en humin*]" Paul writes, "I will live *in them* [*enoikesō en autois*]." Life with God is no longer life lived in proximity to a structure, a Temple, in Jerusalem. In this new era, Paul says that God will dwell *in his followers*. As in 1 Corinthians 3, Jerusalem is not explicitly being dismissed, but the language of Paul is remarkable coming from a Jew for whom the Temple was central to life and thought.

Finally there is 2 Thessalonians 2.3–4. Even though this is a highly disputed letter, it nevertheless represents a disposition reminiscent of Paul in his other letters. Echoing much in Daniel, the passage refers to two events that precede the Second Coming of Christ: a rebellion and the rise of the "man of lawlessness." While much is unclear about the prediction, this "one destined for destruction" (Gk *ho huios tēs apōleias*) not only promotes himself but "takes his seat in the *temple of God*." The best interpretations see this as a reference to the Jerusalem Temple and it echoes Paul's dim view of the Temple elsewhere: in his eschatological schema, the Temple plays a role only in its desecration.

None of these three texts overtly exclude or invalidate the work of the Temple. But they do imply a remarkable departure from the thinking of Paul's day. In an age when the Temple was standing in all of its Herodian glory, Paul could point elsewhere and find in the Church and its people a place that functioned as the Temple functioned. In other words another location was suitable to Paul as a site for the presence of God. Peter Walker points out that this teaching prepared the early Christians for the devastation of the Temple in AD 70. "Paul was laying a secure foundation for the Church should it ever need to exist in a Temple-less age, ensuring that the center of its life was no longer the Temple but Christ himself."[27]

Summary

When Paul's theology moved away from ethnicity and regionalism and focused on personal appropriation of faith and attachment to Christ – a move that was necessary for his Gentile mission – Paul *inevitably* had to abandon a Christian commitment to Jewish territorialism. This explains his lack of interest in any form of divine geography, or any instinct to list the land among the benefits of Judaism. Paul universalizes faith in Christ in order to include all people; Paul universalizes the promises to Abraham in order to include all lands. Indeed for Paul, something new and revolutionary was afoot when Judaism's messianic community was born after Pentecost.

This new openness continued in the Pauline tradition and appears indirectly in Ephesians 6 (a letter with a contested claim to authorship). Here among the list of household rules for Christians, Paul (or one of his followers) cites the fifth commandment about honoring parents. However, the command in Exodus 20.12 comes with a promise. The Old Testament text says that those who so honor their mother and father "will live long in the land the LORD your God is giving you." Remarkably Ephesians 6.2 anchors its moral charge to the Old Testament command and applies the promise to Christian parents. "Honor your father and your mother – this is the first commandment with a promise – that it may be well with you and that you may live long on the land (Gk *epi tes gēs*)." The Old Testament link is clearly to the Land of Promise in Judea and yet here this letter can refer the promise to Ephesian Gentiles and their life in their land. The writer of this letter hardly had in mind a promise that the Ephesians would live long in the Land of Promise in Judea. The notion of "land" has here expanded and now embraces a wider theological geography.

Paul's belief that Abraham was promised "the world" fits with Luke's understanding of the new mission of the Church. The restoration of Judea or the political application of theological promise would not be a part of Christian mission (Acts 1.6–8). The world – as far as Rome – is now within the domain of God's interest and work. This close connection between Luke and Paul should not surprise us. As co-workers, Paul and Luke no doubt discussed these matters at length and the result was a theological outlook void of regional or political ambitions.

Paul's ongoing commitment to his ancestral Judaism in Romans 11 has puzzled his interpreters for generations. Some have viewed it as mere sentimentality. Others as a contradiction deep in the apostle's thinking. Still others as an inconsistency, a slip that Paul felt helpless to avoid. Perhaps it is best to see this commitment as stemming from Paul's understanding of divine sovereignty, covenant, and grace. For God to abandon his Jewish people in their intransigence would invalidate Paul's higher commitment to his view of God and his mercy – not simply for Jews, but for Christians as well. Still again, Paul may have looked at the Mediterranean world, seen the rapid growth of the Church among the Gentiles, and anticipated attitudes that one day would be labeled as "anti-Jewish." By the late first century such attitudes had become a reality. For Christian teaching, Romans 11 should stand opposed to any such ideas.

Many Christian interpreters look at the way Paul has rethought Jewish election in Romans 9—11, seen the prospect of "supersession-ism,"[28] feared the charge of "anti-Semitism" and beaten a hasty retreat from a consistent Pauline theology. Such anxieties are misplaced. Paul has said that Judaism without the Messiah is beloved thus avoiding the horrendous anti-Semitism of later centuries. Paul's own eschat-ology intertwines the fate of Judaism and the fate of the Christian Gentile whose mission should lead to the final inclusion of all Jews. Most treatments of these chapters stress either mercy or judgment on Judaism. But as Paul writes, both are necessary (Rom. 11.22, "Note then the kindness and the severity of God"). Paul blesses Israel but also thinks that unbelieving Jews are not actually all right as they are. What separates Paul from supersessionism is that for him, his fellow Jews are not "debarred in virtue of their ethnic origin from coming back into the family, their own family, that has been renewed in the gospel."[29] God has retained a vital role for Israel in salvation history and anticipates a day when belief in the Messiah Jesus will be discovered.

But certainly Paul would have been surprised, shocked even, if he learned that Christians in Corinth or Ephesus had taken up a Holy Land theology akin to his former rabbinic friends in Jerusalem. Paul would have been surprised if Christian churches began to reflect a Jewish outlook on territorialism. Indeed, Christians were connected to the great ancestor Abraham by faith and by virtue of this, they had joined the family of God. But at no time did these Christians contemplate the implications of the land promises of Abraham.

As Jewish nationalism began to swell in the 50s and 60s, some among Paul's churches might have been tempted to see this call of religious patriotism – a call to defend *holy land* – as a requirement for Christians. Paul would have stopped such sentiments forcefully. The lens of the incarnation had now refocused things completely. Christian theology had no room for "holy places" outside of the Holy One who is Christ. And above all, Paul would have seen as aberrant any *Christian* territorialism wed to first-century politics. A religiously fueled regional nationalism did arise in the first century in Judaism and it eventually delivered Jerusalem to the Roman armies. But nothing of its type ever surfaced in Paul's churches thanks to the apostle's instruction.

7

Developments beyond Paul

Any casual reconstruction of early Christianity's view of the land based on the later books of the New Testament would lead to some surprising results. The Pauline and Johannine traditions were fully engaged in debates about Christian identity *in comparison* with Jewish life. And this led to theological arguments about Abraham, promises given to him, and the security of an identity rooted in lineage. "Abraham *is* our father" becomes the sort of refrain heard in John 8.39 but could also be an echo of sentiments heard as Christians debated Jews in AD 75 or 80. Jesus' response, "*If you were* Abraham's children…" is precisely the sort of retort the Church might have used since it was making its own claim on Abraham. That Abraham became "the father of *many nations*…" not only belongs to Romans 4.18, but was the plea of a Gentile Church instructed by Paul that believed Christians were now heirs of something that had belonged to Judaism.

The Pauline and Johannine communities were busy rethinking the nature of religious identity in comparison with that found in Judaism and they decided that many of the historic categories needed to change. Not only was a connection with Abraham and the historic people of God universalized (inviting Gentiles into the Church) but religious territorialism – a zealous commitment to the land based on religious privilege – would necessarily change with it. Paul's treatment of Jerusalem and the Temple make this clear. Likewise his surprising reinterpretation of the land suggests the same. For instance, Abraham was promised *the world* (Rom. 4.13), not the land of Judea. The scope of religious geography had been permanently altered in Christian consciousness.

When we step outside these traditions, some of these debates disappear. The documents associated with the author of Hebrews, James, Peter, John, Jude – even the Apocalypse itself – demonstrate a striking neglect for concerns over land and conventional holy space.

I say "conventional" because most of them do invest in a locale for Christian hope: heaven or heavenly renewal of this world.[1] And in the Apocalypse, heaven will bring its properties to the earth for its final renewal. In these writings, conventional religious geography *on earth* per se slips from view. In fact it becomes an impediment to the deeper realization that a "better country" awaits the believer who is trusting in God.

Three ideas surface again and again in these books. First, there is no discussion of Judea or Jerusalem as the site of ultimate commitment, affection, or veneration. Jerusalem and its Temple are seen with suspicion, and discussions such as those in Hebrews or the Apocalypse point to the inadequacies of anything going on at the Temple. The "city of God" has now been relocated to something newly built by God and struggle for the city in Judea is abandoned. This view may have resulted from the final destruction of Jerusalem in AD 70 when both Christians and Jews were forced to rethink the meaning of the land much as Augustine was forced to do following the Visigoth sack of Rome in 410. But such a conclusion is unnecessary since these books could well have stemmed from before 70. The Christian theological detachment from Jerusalem was already well underway before the Roman armies arrived at the Holy City.

Second, the worldview of these Christians is the worldview of the exile. "To the exiles of the Dispersion," writes 1 Peter 1.1. "To the twelve tribes in the Dispersion," records James 1.1. Peter implores his followers to follow a moral life, calling them "aliens and exiles" (1 Pet. 2.11) and reminds them that the life lived now is that of an exile (1.17). Christianity has here adopted one motif from its Jewish roots and developed it eagerly: as Israel lived without a land both in Egypt and in Babylon, so too, Christians are likewise landless. Thus the Apocalypse uses Babylon as its reigning symbol for the imperial world that persecutes the Church. In its litany of those who have been faithful, Hebrews describes generic experiences that merge the historic to the present. Believers have been stoned, beaten, imprisoned, left destitute, and found wandering "in deserts and mountains," living in "caves and holes in the ground" (Heb. 11.37–38). They have "taken refuge" (6.18a). Nevertheless, these exiles have hope (6.18b). But the Church replaced the Jewish hope of a Holy Land and its "rest" with a new hope for heavenly rest provided uniquely by God.

This leads us to the third and final element characteristic of these letters. They build a worldview that is at the same time deeply invested in the practicalities of life in the empire and yet is also profoundly eschatological. *They live in this world and yet they have their eyes on another.* They do indeed have hope but it is not invested in the political restoration of Judea or the reform of the empire. They continue to be exiles. They do not talk about the re-establishment of a Jewish nation independent of Rome nor do they see events in Judea as critical to the realization of this hope. They have an eschatology but its key elements center on Christ and the world – not Judaism and Jerusalem.

The book of Hebrews

While this letter (or sermon) has an uncertain setting, we can be sure that its author comes from a Jewish background, believes that Jesus is not only Messiah but Son of God, and now must challenge his readers to rethink the validity of their ancestral Judaism in light of Christian faith. It is difficult to know if he is writing from the Diaspora (Alexandria perhaps) or Jerusalem itself. And perhaps this does not matter. But what is clear is that the letter is working strenuously to reforge the principal legacies of Judaism and warn Jewish Christians not to return to them.

Peter Walker has definitively established that Jerusalem and the Temple are not tangential to this letter's outlook.[2] Attention to the Temple (referred to strategically as the tent or Tabernacle, Gk *skēnē*, ten times) is extensive. And while Hebrews does not fail to recognize the legitimacy of the Tabernacle established with Moses, still, "something greater than Moses" has arrived in Christ (3.3–6). The contrast between the new and the old is proffered again and again. For example, Christ is superior to every high priest not simply because he belongs to an eternal order (Melchizedek, 7.1–28), but because he offered a sacrifice far better than they, a sacrifice of his own life (7.27; 9.12, 26). Moreover, Jesus serves at a Temple that exceeds the earthly Temple and its limitations (8.1–6) just as he oversees a new covenant (an "eternal covenant" 13.20) which makes the former covenant obsolete (8.6, 13). As Son of God he is enthroned at God's right hand (1.3), serves a more perfect "tent" (9.11), and has entered into *this* Holy Place, taking his own blood as a superior sacrifice (9.12–14). Immediately the thrust of this sort of argument is evident:

given the incarnation, the present religious structures that Judaism promoted have become redundant.

Walker concludes that "this is a sweeping conclusion for any Jewish writer" and it compares favorably with the sermon given by Stephen in Acts 8.[3] The earthly sanctuary begun with the Tabernacle and continued in the Temple has found its fulfillment in Christ. What was once vital is now shown to be provisional and, finally, unnecessary. So Hebrews explains in 10.11 that the daily sacrifices of the priest *can never take away sin*. This is astounding. In such a breathtaking theological framework, it would make sense that yet another legacy of Judaism – the land – would likewise meet abrupt comparisons.

The city of God

Hebrews is fully aware of the importance of Jerusalem in Jewish consciousness. And yet the letter deflects interest from this city to a heavenly city prepared by God. "For here we have no lasting city, but we are looking for the city that is to come" (13.14). In 7.1 when we meet Melchizedek, he is described as coming from "Salem." In the first century this was identified with Jerusalem based on Psalm 76.2 (also in Josephus, *Antiquities*, 1.180, "afterward they called Salem Jerusalem"). And while Hebrews surely knows this tradition, it does not refer to it. This may be because Hebrews wishes to point our interest elsewhere to a heavenly Jerusalem, a city built by God. Melchizedek's defining city is in heaven – not an earthly city.

Hebrews refers to "the city" four times, and in each case, the reference is to a heavenly city (11.10, 16; 12.22; 13.14). Such a city was even the aspiration of Abraham, who sought a "city that has no foundations, whose architect and builder is God" (11.10). In 12.22 Hebrews overturns the language of Jewish pilgrimage in a similar way. The cycle of Jewish festival life as well as the framework of Jewish faith itself aimed the believing Jew toward the Temple and it made Jerusalem the one locale of pilgrimage. But now, Hebrews writes, the *heavenly Jerusalem* is the destination of people of faith. He refers to both the Temple ("Mount Zion") and the city itself ("the city of the living God") as now the new pilgrim destination of the believer.[4]

The effect of this on the believer who was located far from Jerusalem must have been astounding. This holy geography was accessible from any province or city. Therefore by relocating the true Jerusalem, Hebrews undercuts any need for literal pilgrimage to Judea. For

Christians today who have a limited appreciation for pilgrimage destinations and for whom pilgrimage is not a part of their religious vocabulary or experience, such an adjustment would seem trivial. But for a territorial religion like Judaism it was enormous. No longer is a geographical *place* a destination of religious faithfulness.

In the book's final chapter, Hebrews offers perhaps the most provocative explanation of the Christian's disposition regarding Jerusalem. After warning its readers against religious meals designed to evoke some connection to Jerusalem's sacrifices, Hebrews says that we possess an alternative altar from which the priests who serve at the tent have no right to eat. Then we are taken on an important detour: "For the bodies of those animals whose blood is brought into the sanctuary by the high priest as a sacrifice for sin are burned outside the camp. Therefore Jesus also suffered outside the city gate in order to sanctify the people by his own blood. Let us then go to him outside the camp and bear the abuse he endured" (13.11–13). In this image, Jesus has joined the carcasses of the sacrificed animals at the Temple in a place of defilement *outside the city.* And yet, ironically, Jesus has made that which was unholy the locale of true holiness. Hebrews then enjoins us: *Let us go outside the camp.* In other words, in order to join the heavenly Jerusalem, something must be left behind – the old Jerusalem must be exited – in order to join Jesus who himself had no part of the city itself in his death.

If Jerusalem is no longer a destination for Christian affection, surely Hebrews would say the same about the land. Here the argument is linked to the one man in whom land promise was well known: Abraham.

The hope of Abraham: a better country

We have seen the centrality of the traditions surrounding Abraham and the land throughout the New Testament and Judaism. Hebrews is aware of these. Abraham is the archetype of faith and the recipient of the two promises of God: progeny (or nation) and land. And yet it is the subtle changes to this tradition that betray this writer's intention. In 6.13–15 the promise to Abraham is reviewed and we learn that there is but one promise: "I will bless you and multiply you." This is half the promise.

In chapter 11 Hebrews explores the second aspect of the promise. By faith Abraham moved toward "the Land of Promise" as if it were a foreign land (11.9). *Foreign land?* This is both irony and foreshadowing. Indeed Canaan was foreign to Abraham because he was from Ur. But more is meant: this land is foreign at a deeper level – it is merely a shadow of the genuine promise God wants to give. This is the Holy Land, the land destined as an inheritance for himself, Isaac and Jacob. And yet in an unexpected development, Hebrews says that Abraham died *without* ever receiving the promise (11.13, 39). Abraham moved from Mesopotamia to Canaan and walked in the Land of Promise. There is no question that he recognized that this land was to be his land. After he passes through Shechem and Moreh, the LORD tells him, "To your offspring I will give *this* land" (Gen. 12.7) and in response Abraham builds an altar there. From Shechem Abraham continues south to Bethel and then on south to Hebron before he departs for Beersheba in the Negev and Egypt. After Abraham has walked the entire land, God confirms his promise with a covenant and a recital of the land's geographical particulars (Gen. 15.17–21). At the end of the Abraham saga, Sarah is buried in the land (Gen. 23.19) as is Abraham himself (Gen. 25.9–10), and their tombs were well-known in Hebron even to the first century.

It is specious to suggest that when Hebrews says "Abraham did not receive the land" it is referring to Abraham's failure to completely control the land in settlement. He lived alongside the Canaanites but nevertheless knew that this land was his by divine promise. Nevertheless, Hebrews intimates that the deeper meaning of the promise to Abraham did not have to do with the territory between Shechem and Beersheba. This is because throughout his life of wandering his eye had been set on a different city – a different land – that was to be built by God (11.10). For Hebrews the land is simply a foretaste, a metaphor perhaps, of a more profound location with God. If this is true Hebrews can reach the following deduction: Abraham continued to be a stranger and alien on the earth (or in the land?) despite his life in the Land of Promise (11.13). "Alien" (Gk *parepidēmos*) is the very term Peter uses for his Christian audience in the Diaspora. In a word, Abraham has joined the ranks of the alien Christians in Hebrews' worldview. Abraham walked in the land as if it were a Diaspora.

Ironically even though Abraham stood in Shechem, Bethel, and Hebron, Hebrews can say that the patriarch only saw the land and greeted it from afar (11.13). How can this be true? Because Abraham sought something greater: a homeland (11.14, Gk *patris*). This is the only use of this word in the New Testament letters (cf. Mark 6.1; Luke 4.23; etc.) and its appearance here is poignant. In Jewish writing it refers to the land given by God, the Holy Land, that could be lost in exile or death (Jer. 22.10; 2 Macc. 13.10). But Hebrews says that our "homeland" has changed. It is not on the earth. The argument is sustained in 11.16 where Hebrews continues, "But as it is, they long for a better *patris* – which belongs to heaven." Believers yearn for a "better country" where the greatest promises of God might be found.

The aim of Moses: God's rest

The second Old Testament narrative used extensively in Hebrews comes from the story of Israel's departure from Egypt and arrival in the Land of Promise under Joshua. Since the book's aim is a sustained exhortation for its readers to retain faith and not regress, this narrative dramatically illustrates the consequences of unbelief. The generation that left Egypt died in the wilderness with hardened hearts (3.17; 4.7). They never entered the land with Joshua.

Throughout the Old Testament, the obvious destination of the Israelites after their exodus from Egypt was the land promised to the patriarchs. After their 40-year journey in the wilderness Moses led Israel to the mountains east of the Jordan river and from here Joshua guided them across the Jordan river with another great parting of the water. They then stepped into the Promised Land for the first time. So much is clear. The land was the destination and hope of Israel.

The author of Hebrews knows this story as intimately as any Jewish writer could. It is the salvation-narrative of Israel. Joshua's conquest and occupation of the land served as a template for the territorialism that stirred Judea throughout the Hellenistic era. However, Hebrews contours this tradition to say something different. Throughout the book of Numbers (see 14.21–24) the consequence of disbelief is that the wandering Israelite would not "see the land" sworn to the patriarchs. On the other hand, those that had faith and obeyed would "enter the land." Hebrews 3.7–11 cites Psalm 95.7–11 (LXX 94.7–11) in order to reinterpret the goal of Israel's Old Testament pilgrimage. Psalm 95.11 says that God was bringing Israel into his "rest." Hebrews capitalizes on this term and replaces the land with it.

Throughout the summary of the Moses–Joshua story in Hebrews 3—4, "rest" (Gk *katapausis*) occurs eight times without any reference to the land. This is the new pilgrimage of the people of God and it is modeled by the pilgrimage of Old Testament Israel. We move from Egypt to God's rest (4.1) precisely as Israel did. However, the aim of this journey, indeed the destination of this pilgrimage, is never a place, never a geographical location: it is salvation provided by God. Hebrews even combines the use of "rest" in Psalm 95 with the command for Sabbath rest found in Genesis 2.2 to give greater definition to the Christian hope (4.4). The pilgrim moves toward "God's rest" (4.9–10) where all labor will cease.

This reconfiguration of pilgrimage destination fits securely with the comparison that Hebrews plays out continually between Moses and Christ.[5] The comparison that began in 3.3 takes final form in the last chapters of the book. In 12.18–24 dramatic comparisons are made between historic Mount Sinai (with its fire, warnings, and tremors) and the heavenly Mount Zion (with its angels, festive array, and Jesus as mediator). We simply are to think of Christ as another Moses leading believers to a new destination. In 13.20 God does not "raise up" Christ from the dead: God "leads up" (Gk *anagō*) Christ using the same language of Moses' "leading up" Israel out of Egypt (Exod. 33.15; Num. 14.13). Just like Moses, Jesus is another shepherd (13.20b) who now is taking his people to a new land, a heavenly land, a "better country" (11.16).

Revelation

This final book of the New Testament (also called the Apocalypse, meaning the "unveiling") presents a bewildering array of problems for our topic not found elsewhere. Even its author and its origin are uncertain. The book is credited to John (1.4) but is this the same as the author of the Fourth Gospel? Is this another John, someone called "the elder"? Is this John the Baptist? Scholars are divided.

Revelation does not offer a straightforward history of early Christian behavior or reflections concerning the land. Instead it employs numerous cryptic symbols that have defied interpreters since it was penned. It thus presents a unique New Testament genre and as such demands unique interpretive tactics. This is Jewish-Christian apocalyptic that has much in common with the "little apocalypse" found in the synoptic Gospels (Mark 13). It also is similar to an array of other apocalyptic writings from the same period.[6]

Following seven letters to churches located in Asia Minor, Revelation introduces us to John's visionary experience of God's throne similar to that of Isaiah (6.1), Ezekiel (1.1), and Daniel (7.1). After a full description of this scene, John's focus narrows to the Lamb who was slain and who holds a sealed scroll that, when unfurled, reveals God's final program for the world (5.6–14). Seven seals are followed by unfolding series of seven (or six according to some scholars): trumpets, signs, bowls, etc., each demonstrating God's sovereignty and judgment that is now due on the earth. The great climax comes at the revealing of the harlot in 17—18 who is judged and killed: this inaugurates the triumph of God and the final resolution of evil in the world.

While most scholars today agree that the clues to the book are found in Old Testament, Jewish apocalyptic writing and Qumran, most are unsure about the best interpretative approach for the book. Today three models are generally in use.[7] (1) For *preterists* (Latin *praeter*, or past) the controlling metaphors of the book need to come from the circumstances surrounding the mid-first century, particularly the fall of Jerusalem in AD 70. In this case, its various creatures and catastrophes point to players such as Vespasian and Nero, Rome and Jerusalem, that would have been recognized immediately by the book's first readers. Thus the eagle in chapter 8, the beast from the sea in 13.1, as well as the "seven hills" of 17.9 might refer to Rome. And the fall of Babylon may well echo Amos 5.2, where the Old Testament city is a metaphor for the generation in Jerusalem that has repudiated God and the law. This method simply suggests that the descriptions in the book are keyed to events surrounding John himself and the predictions within its pages were fulfilled in the first century.

(2) Others who could be labeled *futurists* argue that the prophetic character of the book and its description of the end of human history point to a time not known by the author. However, this has led to remarkable and unpersuasive interpretations of images that are as striking as they are unbelievable. Charlemagne, Mussolini, Hitler, and Mikhail Gorbachev as well as the Roman Catholic Church and the Protestant Reformation have all been located in its pages. Even the seven heads and ten horns on the dragon of 12.3 (cf. 17.16) have been interpreted as the European Union. (Preterists, by contrast, are content to find in these symbolic kingdoms empires that

preceded Rome.) The problem with this approach is interpretative control. Revelation becomes a book barely understood by John and marginally relevant to his circumstances. And additionally each new generation in this futurist tradition has deemed *their time* as holding the hermeneutical key.

(3) Still others are *idealists* who see in the book a timeless symbolism that should speak to every generation. Here are principles that demonstrate ideals of spiritual struggle that ultimately will lead to divine victory. Revelation is a drama depicting classic ancient images of beasts and dragons who represent evil in its many cosmic and political forms. Its message is clear: God is in control of history and no matter the force of evil, God will prevail.[8]

A synthesis of the first and third approaches is best. Revelation offers a sweeping theatrical panorama of the struggle between God and a violent, sinful world. And yet its primary audience in John's day would find in it clues that suggest the turmoil and struggle of their time will find resolution if hope is placed in God. In some cases the clues are located in the Old Testament, where Ezekiel and Daniel are guides. Or they evoke memories of plagues found in Moses' confrontation with Pharaoh. In other cases they hint at circumstances directly related to the first century. On occasion the meaning seems clear: veiled allusions to Rome abound. On other occasions interpretations are very uncertain – such as the meaning of Babylon or the great harlot. Perhaps the classic text for this uncertainty is 13.16–18, the mark of the beast. "This calls for wisdom:" John writes, "let anyone with understanding calculate the number of the beast, for…its number is six hundred and sixty-six." Clearly John is hinting that his readers need to discern this meaning – but even Irenaeus writing just over 100 years later was at a loss. Ford provides a detailed and fascinating history of the many, many ways this number has been interpreted, and it leads to one conclusion: we really do not know. Idealists typically would simply let 666 be a generic symbol for imperfection and failure.[9]

Revelation and Judea

Amidst the many uncertainties that surround this book, one thing is clear: John's vision concerns God's resolution for the entire world and never Judea. The term "land" occurs in this book a remarkable 82 times (one-third of all New Testament occurrences) and in each case it points to the earth and never to the Holy Land. In 5.3 we learn that no one in heaven or on earth can open the scroll. In 5.13 John hears the singing of every creature in heaven and on earth. In 6.15 we read about the kings of the earth (also 16.14; 17.2; 18.3, 9; 19.19). In 7.1 the four angels stand at the four corners of the earth holding back the "four winds of the earth." In chapter 10 the angel reading the scroll straddles the sea and the earth. In John's view, God is here bringing redemption and judgment to the entire world in its widest capacity, never the limited land of Judea. In chapter 14, an angel typically calls out to all residents of this world, "Fear God and give him glory, because the hour of his judgment has come. Worship him who made the heaven and earth, the sea and the springs of water."

John's interest in Judea is focused on Jerusalem and enjoys marked attention in chapter 11. This is the "holy city" where the "Lord was crucified" (11.2, 8). And yet this is not a site of hope or redemption for God's people. The two witnesses who speak to the city are killed violently (11.7) by the "beast that comes up," and this results in a catastrophic earthquake that judges the city and ruins much of it (11.13). The hope of Jerusalem is not here in the city nicknamed Sodom and Egypt (11.8). The hope for Jerusalem is found in the heavenly Jerusalem that descends in chapter 21 to take its place. Walker correctly writes, "There is no encouragement to believe that the earthly Jerusalem might somehow be metamorphosed into the heavenly one."[10] The climactic scene of the book displays the judgment of the violent and unbelieving systems of this world; Jerusalem is counted among them. Contrary to the accepted teaching within Judaism, the human restoration of Jerusalem or Judea plays no role in the restoration of the earth.

Most interpreters see genuine allusions to the fall of Jerusalem in AD 70. Thus John may be writing in order to make sense of this catastrophe just as similar Jewish apocalypses were forced to do (cf. *2 Baruch, 4 Ezra*). And if this is true, Rome's conquest of the city is also a divine judgment on it. However, this destruction also alludes to the destruction of another city later in the book – Babylon – which for some may also refer to Jerusalem, but also alludes to Rome itself. Here we meet "the great harlot" (17.1) who rides a scarlet beast with seven heads and ten horns. John explains that the seven heads refer to "seven hills" (17.9), which certainly points to Rome. "They are also seven kings," John writes, and the most satisfying interpretation sees them as veiled allusions to Rome's violent and chaotic mid-first-century history.

But it may be that the harlot refers to Jerusalem or the high priest in his final corruption before the war. Josephus describes how the Zealots who took the city appointed their own priest, which led to innumerable abominations echoing those of Revelation 17 (*Wars*, 6.151–192). But also the harlot bears on her forehead "a name, a mystery" (17.5), which is an ironic echo of the high priest's inscribed gold plate ("Holy to the LORD," Exod. 28.36–38). And the martyrdoms of 17.6 may point to Jerusalem which killed the prophets (cf. 18.24). Babylon is her name – and Babylon now has become Jerusalem which is burned (18.9) and leads to the wailing of many. Is Jerusalem the "great city" (18.18)? Indeed. In Jewish apocalyptic and commentary, Jerusalem was the center of the world. The harlot who rides the beast is the dramatic image of defilement and the ultimate subject of judgment. Together their history was a history that cost many Christians their lives (17.6) and "they will make war on the Lamb" (17.14).

But is not Babylon also referring to Rome? It is. But here is the key: What befell Jerusalem will also befall Rome. Jerusalem has become a paradigm which Rome will serve. John envisions the judgment of Rome and shapes that vision by the memory of Jerusalem's devastation. "The great city will be thrown down" (18.21) is the harrowing judgment on human history. The harps and the flutes and the trumpets will go silent (18.22). The violent and pagan corruptions of this world now stand before their Christ. "The kingdom of the world has become the kingdom of our Lord" (11.15). "The Lamb will conquer them for he is Lord of lords and King of kings" (17.14).

Revelation and hope

There is no sense in Revelation that Christians are to invest in or fight for the restoration or preservation of Jerusalem in the climactic scenario of the Last Days. Attachment to Judea or affection for the land do not figure in John's outlook. Safety cannot be found in a place, much less the Temple or city of Jerusalem. The Holy City is not a place of yearning – for even its Temple is doomed (11.1–2). This is not an eschatology that is keyed to the politics of Judea except to say that these politics have been corrupted and now must be overruled by God himself. The paradigm of judgment is for the earth, for all cities – Jerusalem and Rome – which have brought evil and violence to God's creation. The fall of Jerusalem was a foretaste of what could happen elsewhere.

The hope of Revelation is in God's eschatological intervention. Hope is found in the descent of the new Jerusalem (21.2) that will take up where the former Jerusalem had failed. Hope is found not in the destruction of the world but in the renewal of the world when God's will is done. Where God dwells with humanity, they truly become his people and every tear is wiped away (21.3–4).

To fight for holy territory, to defend the land as a divinely appointed duty, is to regress utterly in the most miserable way. It is to misplace hope entirely. The kingdoms of this world will be judged. And this includes the kingdom of Judea. Hope in Revelation is for a "new heaven and a new earth" (21.1) that reorders creation as it ought to be.

Conclusion

What is the basis of hope in these writings? Certainly Hebrews has not entirely adopted a Greek dualism that denies any hope for this world. We continue to live in this world – indeed in "the Empire" – and God notes carefully our life and progress in it. Moreover, Hebrews urges us to go "outside" the city (13.13) and seek the "city that is to come" (13.14). This is the language of exile – the language of political detachment, a perspective that will not valorize the value-systems of the world and yet places all hope in God. This is Jewish eschatology that does not simply dismiss the world, but looks for what God is preparing to do for it. We are urged that the cities and kingdoms found in this world are uncertain and are no place to locate hope. Here we have "no lasting city" (13.14). Hebrews wants us to seek an unshakable kingdom, a permanent city, a better country built by God.

If there were any doubts that a thoughtful critique of territorial theology was at work among the early Christians, Hebrews puts them to rest. The author of this book and those who embraced its understanding of the world would never be inclined to see the politics of Judea as an appropriate venue for Christian interest. Nor would they anticipate a divine reclamation of Judea or a revival in Jerusalem as a component of their eschatology. Their call: *"We seek a better country"* – a *patris*, a homeland which God alone is going to build.

Revelation takes this understanding further. Revelation spins an apocalyptic drama that demonstrates the bankruptcy of this world – including Jerusalem and Judea – and the costs incurred by believers who have resisted it. This is the language not only of exile but of martyrdom (17.6). In Revelation it is the Holy Land that becomes a land of violence toward the people of God and in the end is subject to judgment and devastation. Revelation does not look to the land as an object of hope and promise. *The great city is torn down.* Instead Jerusalem's future will only be secured when God builds it anew and those who have had designs on it are defeated. When heaven descends to earth and a "better country" is born.

One of the chief problems with the idealist interpretation of Revelation is that it empties the book of Revelation of one of its central messages. In a word, it does not treat the Apocalypse as apocalyptic. For some, the drama is distilled down to a simple message of hope: the violent of this world stand under God's judgment; nevertheless God loves the world and will do anything to intervene and bring righteousness and justice. This much is true but it says too little. Revelation provides a theological framework that declares the tragedy of human history and the impossibility of humanity rescuing itself from that tragedy. No political, religious, or economic system will ultimately cure the world of its ills. The violent carry the world where they will. The better country will not be built by its occupants. No military campaign to rid the world of darkness and no ideology to reorganize the world will bring the relief God's people seek. Such resolution, such final resolution, will only be found when God himself declares his judgment on human history, redeems those whose hearts seek his mercy, and at last brings his kingdom to bear on the kingdoms of this world with all its power and glory.

There is no room in Revelation for religious nostalgia, for sentiments that want to rebuild what once was promised for the land in Old Testament history. There is no call for renewal as if humanity could find its political or historical redemption *from within* Judea's boundaries. But there is an explicit warning to all "Babylons." The violent and impious have been put on notice. This is God's world and not our own. Humanity's cities or empires have a limited tenure and are weighed in the balance.

Religious territorialism in this framework is at best ironic. It could be compared with children squabbling over the desserts as the *Titanic* approaches its destiny. The wider perspective of Revelation is for the world, not the land, and what God has determined to do for it.

8

Land, theology, and the Church

To think Christianly about land – in particular, the *Land of Promise* – we have to remind ourselves how central land is to our understanding of reality, history, even our view of God's creation. Whenever we conceptualize land we are engaging in a *social construct*, expressing our values and our theologies about ownership and our place in this world with God. For some cultures, land is sacred and a gift from God. And our lives are woven into the fabric of the life found in the land. For others, land is something to be subjugated, tamed, and owned. In the introduction to his book on land ideologies in the Old Testament, the Australian scholar Norman Habel compares the Western view of land with that of the Aborigines of Australia: "For Aboriginal Australians the land is sacred, filled with ancestral dreamings that determine kinship, sacred site, and ceremony. All species of life, including humans, are bound to the land. Land does not belong to people; people belong to land."[1]

Habel then compares this with the Western European explorer for whom land is terrain to be conquered. For him, "land is arid desert, fierce jungle, or awesome mountain. As such, land is a challenge, a new horizon for human reason to dominate and a fearsome encounter with mortality. Land is territory for managing and mapping. Once land is on the map, the explorer turns entrepreneur and re-conquers the land as a vast economic resource."[2]

The biblical tradition is no stranger to these interests. We have seen how the Old Testament, early Judaism, and the New Testament wrestled in their own ways with the question of divinely promised land. The Holy Land – the land promised to Abraham and his descendants – became both the great gift and the great temptation of Israel. To echo the categories of Brueggemann, Israel continually had to make a moral choice: to grasp the land with force or to wait for the land as gift. The first viewed land as a right and all challengers were to be vanquished. The second viewed it as a privilege, something to be shared among the poor and strangers, something originating from God and so demanding restraint and humility.

Soon in the Hellenistic era (the time of the New Testament), the land became the source of enormous debate. Many rabbis reaffirmed the Old Testament promises as uniquely Jewish and upheld the ideology of grasping. Others disagreed vigorously. Some promoted a religious territoriality that evolved into unrelenting demands for territorial privilege. Others were wary of where such territorialism might lead.

But as we have seen, Jesus and his followers refused to support the territoriality of the Jewish leaders of Judea. Judaism under the Roman occupation leaned heavily on its legacy of their land promises, called for resistance and struggle, and, in the end, lost the land to Roman armies. And yet still other Jews questioned whether this land theology was fully appropriate. Diaspora Judaism launched a theoretical debate that was only silenced on the other side of war.

Today these debates continue in our contemporary setting. In many cases they are shaped by the same theological concerns of the biblical period. In other cases they spring from the politics of the modern Middle East and the struggle of cultures to survive there. Jews living in New York City or London (two modern Diasporas) might find themselves debating with Jerusalem's orthodox Jews about the necessity of living in modern Israel in order to pursue a life fully in keeping with the law. And Christians in San Antonio, Texas, or in Glasgow, Scotland, might well argue that the land promises of Abraham are still in play today in the Middle East and the failure to respect them will lead to spiritual and national jeopardy.

But we must be clear. Just as Judaism and Christianity debated the merits of the land in their early centuries within their own ranks, the same is true today. Not all Jews have a territorial theology. Nor do all Christians. However just as in the first century, these ancient debates have arisen again. In modern Israel the settler movement represents this well. And among Christians, a movement called Christian Zionism has developed these views for the masses.

A short narrative from my own experience will illustrate what it looks like when these movements are encountered. It will sound extreme – which it is. And these voices do not represent the mainstream of the Christian community. But they are nevertheless potent forces which have reignited the ancient debates.

A conversation in Jerusalem

In the early 1990s, I was visiting an evangelical college located on the shoulder of Mount Zion called Jerusalem University College (formerly the Institute of Holy Land Studies). I was having lunch with a table of American evangelical pastors and teachers and, as often happens, the conversation evolved into questions about theology and Israel. A Palestinian uprising was in full swing and so I asked the table, "So what do you think of Israel and the Palestinian uprising?"

Across from me sat an evangelical pastor who said with clear-eyed conviction, "I think that the Bible tells us what should happen. Joshua removed the Canaanites as an act of obedience and faith. The same thing needs to happen today." In other words he was suggesting that we should use the book of Joshua and its pattern of conquest and expulsion to solve the current Arab–Israeli conflict.

I didn't respond but instead waited to see how many at the table would give their consent. And much to my surprise it was agreed by everyone that Joshua offered a credible precedent for Israeli domestic policy today. The Palestinians were interlopers on a land that had been divinely given to modern Israel and any means – even violent means – were appropriate to remove them. These were American evangelical pastors who would return to their pulpits within the week.

This perspective is not uncommon among some Christians. I have heard it for most of my professional life. Sentiments like these are shared by pastors and numerous television preachers today. David Brickner, executive director of the messianic Christian organization Jews for Jesus, echoes them when he writes:

> I believe the modern day state of Israel is a miracle of God and a fulfillment of Bible prophecy. Jesus clearly said that "Jerusalem would be trodden down by the Gentiles until the time of the nations is fulfilled" (Luke 21:24). It has been 50 years since the founding of that state, but only 30 years since Jerusalem came under the control of Jews for the first time since Jesus made that prediction. Could it be that "this generation shall not pass until all these things are fulfilled?"
>
> Peril awaits those who presume to say that God is finished with His chosen people: "And in that day will I make Jerusalem a burdensome stone for all people: all that burden themselves with it shall be cut in

pieces, though all the people of the earth be gathered together against it." (Zechariah 12:3 KJV). Woe to anyone who joins those nations to gather against the Jewish people who are now back in the city of David. Just as God judged the nation of Egypt for her ill treatment of His people, so will He judge nations today. Evangelicals who would understand the Middle East must pay close attention to the teaching of Scripture, and take note of the cosmic forces that now do battle in the heavens but will soon do battle on earth. They must choose carefully which side to uphold.[3]

Here is a Christian territorial theology in full bloom fueled by historical arguments and linked to biblical promises. And today it is living in close connection with some Jewish Zionist movements that share similar themes. These arguments may even echo many of the same theological debates that were tossed about in the Hellenistic era known to Jesus and Paul. And for some, the arguments represent the sentiments of the same Zealots that took Judaism to war with Rome in AD 66.

Modern Jewish Zionism as a territorial ideology came into full force in the late nineteenth century. Initially it was secular but religious motifs were used as a feature of Jewish cultural identity. It was followed by numerous political organizations that viewed the birth of a Jewish state as a cultural and religious mandate. The twentieth century witnessed not only extensive immigrations of Jews into (then) British Palestine but in 1948 the birth of the Jewish state of Israel.

Throughout the twentieth century Christians felt compelled to respond to this movement. For some, this was the fulfillment of prophecy. For others it was a moral correction to what had happened to Jews in Europe. For still others, such territorialism opened a new set of ethical problems. Simply put: the land was already occupied by thousands of Palestinians. Eventually the new Zionists set about photographing and mapping the land while assessing strategies for forcefully expelling the Arab population. (The government working group was "The Committee on Population Transfer.") After the birth of the fledgling state, the government began emptying and destroying over 400 Palestinian villages.

I have already written elsewhere at length about the injustices and violence this sort of thinking has produced in modern Israel in Palestine, in *Whose Land? Whose Promise?*[4] The settler movement in Israel (which today is central to these moral problems) has no end of critics and today is at the heart of renewed tensions between both the United States and European governments and the Israeli government. A comprehensive history and critique of the movement from within Israel has been written by Gershom Gorenberg, *The Accidental Empire: Israel and the Birth of the Settlements, 1967–1977.*[5]

Just as the first-century Church was forced to grapple with Jewish territorialism and nationalism, so too, the Christian Church today must do the same. This is our final assignment. Given what we have seen from the New Testament and its views on the land, it is problematic that today some Christians have reclaimed a territorial theology that appears out of step with what the New Testament teaches. Indeed, these Christians are often intimately linked with the Israeli settler movement. The West Bank city of Hebron (south of Jerusalem) has an Arab population of about 150,000. Yet within its city center are 500 settlers guarded by 1,200 Israeli soldiers. Recently the settlers built a new welcome center for Christian groups who arrive to support their efforts. A visit there shows how theology and politics can be merged in the thinking of both Jewish and Christian communities.

Christian Zionist territorial theology

Within the popular world of evangelicalism, a subgroup exists called Christian Zionists, who have promoted a type of territorial theology that, as I have argued throughout this book, has been foreign to Christianity since its inception. Its history may reach back as far as the Puritans, but its contemporary expression took shape among Christians in Britain and America at the end of the nineteenth century. For the history of Christian Zionism in the West, Stephen Sizer has given us *Christian Zionism: Road-Map to Armageddon?* (2005), which carefully outlines the origins of the movement.[6] That same year, Timothy Weber explained the unusual relationship between these evangelicals and the state of Israel in *On the Road to Armageddon: How Evangelicals Became Israel's Best Friend.*[7] Together these studies combine with many others to develop for us a composite picture of how these evangelicals have framed a worldview for modern Israel.

But for some scholars, Christian Zionism is not about theology at all. Recently Robert O. Smith provided a useful correction:

Christian Zionism isn't simply a collection of beliefs. A person isn't a Christian Zionist only because they believe in the rapture or they happen to be a Christian who, with the majority of Americans, sympathizes with Israel.

Instead, Christian Zionism is best understood as political action, informed by specifically Christian commitments, to promote or preserve Jewish control over the geographic area now containing Israel and the occupied Palestinian territories. Political activity can take many forms, from hosting a pro-Israel rally at a church to circulating petitions to voting.[8]

Smith also reminds us that Christian Zionism is not always about eschatology either. "Not all Christian Zionists are motivated by end-times hopes. Indeed, many are keenly aware of the history of Jewish suffering at Christian hands, especially during the Holocaust. They often feel called by God to help further strengthen the State of Israel to provide a safeguard against future Jewish suffering."[9]

Therefore Christian Zionism knows diversity. But here I would disagree with Smith. Among evangelicals, eschatology often plays a critical role – witness the extensive literature devoted to this theme. Zeal to see the Second Coming of Christ has led them to construct a historical platform upon which the Second Coming might occur. Judaism's recovery of the land is simply a way station to a further goal, and Jews who return to the land will have a shocking surprise awaiting them. Moreover, for a church to sponsor a "pro-Israel" rally, at the least the evangelical tradition should require some biblical justification for the effort.

The history of conservative Christian movements in the United States provides numerous examples of the views that evolved into this eschatologically motivated Zionism. Throughout the nineteenth century Christian pilgrims visited Palestine and were thrilled to witness what they thought was the fulfillment of important biblical promises. I think, for instance, of Revd DeWitt Talmage, who was pastor of the Brooklyn Tabernacle in New York in the mid-nineteenth century and returned home from such a pilgrimage to publish his *Twenty Five Sermons from the Holy Land*. In it he offered a romantic picture of a Jewish renaissance in the country. And he praised philanthropists for financing the return of Jewish life there. For Talmage it was the renewal of something biblical. Here is a sample from one of his sermons:

[Many who are] large-hearted have paid the passage to Palestine for many of the Israelites, and set apart lands for their culture; and it is only a beginning of the fulfillment of Divine prophecy, when these people shall take possession of the Holy land. The road from Joppa to Jerusalem, and all the roads leading to Nazareth and Galilee, we saw lined with processions of Jews, going to the sacred places, either on holy pilgrimage, or as settlers. All the fingers of Providence nowadays are pointing toward that resumption of Palestine by the Israelites.

In 1891 George Adam Smith wrote his popular book *The Historical Geography of the Holy Land* and there portrayed an empty, biblical land awaiting the return of Judaism. Such publications resonated with a growing evangelical interest in Palestine and the Bible and they fueled the perception that something remarkable, something biblical might be fulfilled should Judaism return.

This interest in the Bible was given a solid footing among early evangelists in Britain and the USA. I think particularly of William Blackstone (1841–1935), who was a Chicago evangelist and student of Dwight Moody. In 1878 he published *Jesus is Coming*, which was America's first best-seller that looked at the return of the Jews to the Holy Land and linked it to the Second Coming of Christ. The book went through three editions and was translated into 42 languages. In 1890 Blackstone was visiting Jewish settlements in the Holy Land and organizing prophecy conferences in Chicago to restore Jews to Palestine.

It is a short step from Blackstone to the views presented by today's Christian Zionists. Speakers and writers such as the late Jerry Falwell, Hal Lindsey, Mike Evans, Jan Vander Hoeven, Pat Robertson, Ralph Reed, Tim and Beverly LaHaye, Jack Hayford, Gary Bauer, John Hagee, James Kennedy, and Kay Arthur promote a parallel view of the Middle East. They write books, promote conferences, sponsor websites, and lead large trips to Israel. They are anxious to see the Jewish people re-established in their sacred land. And they see this as a marker that we are living in a terminal generation that will witness the end of time and Christ's return.

Building a Christian territorial theology?

In contrast to the simple eschatology described above, for many other Christian Zionists the eschatological component sits atop what we might call a biblical-theological meta-narrative for Judaism. It is a narrative that promotes a theological cycle centering on the land. And within this cycle there are three principal movements: land promise, land loss, and land recovery. And most importantly – and this is what makes Christian Zionism unique – they believe that this cycle has begun to operate again today. Israel is returning from its loss and is thus in the process of recovery. But there is one more element which Jews who might champion this cycle will find surprising. Christian Zionists have attached to this territorial cycle an eschatology. *This is the final cycle.* And when it is complete, the end of history will come. Four steps build this territorial theology.

Territorial promise

This territorial dimension of Israel's faith is anchored in God's promises to Abraham in Genesis 12, 15, and 17. These land promises are not viewed as spiritual metaphors that can be dispensed or reinterpreted. These are concrete promises of genuine inheritance, genuine territory, genuine real-estate if you will, measured by the names of the nations from whom land will be taken. The text of Genesis 17.7–9 is representative:

> "...I will establish my covenant between me and you, and your offspring after you throughout their generations, for an everlasting covenant, to be God to you and to your offspring after you. And I will give to you, and to your offspring after you, the land where you are now an alien, all the land of Canaan, for a perpetual holding; and I will be their God."
>
> God said to Abraham, "As for you, you shall keep my covenant, you and your offspring after you throughout their generations..."

Note carefully that this is an everlasting promise and not one that will be revoked. It will also be a continuous promise enjoyed not simply by Abraham but by his descendants. But this promise is not for all Abraham's children: the repetition of the Abrahamic promise later in Genesis shows that it is narrowed to Isaac (Gen. 26.2–4) and then to Jacob (28.13–15) and the tribes that will spring from him. In each case, the reiteration of the promise echoes the original promise to Abraham: the inheritance of land will be the hallmark of God's fidelity to his own promise and by extension, it will reflect on the immutability of God's good character.

Christian Zionists take the permanence of such promises seri-ously. Moreover they view those who deny them or perhaps invalidate their use today as profoundly contradicting God's word. Anchored to the promise of land is also a warning repeated often in Christian Zionist literature. It follows God's command that Abraham leave his country and move west: "The LORD said to Abram, 'Go from your country and your kindred and your father's household to the land that I will show you. I will make of you a great nation, and I will bless you, and make your name great, so that you will be a blessing. I will bless those who bless you, and the one who curses you I will curse; and in you all the families of the earth shall be blessed'" (Gen. 12.1–3).

This passage is frequently used as a warning to theologians and political policy-makers today. Genesis 12.2 almost stands alone: "I will bless those who bless you, and the one who curses you I will curse." Those who are obstacles to this promise, who deny to Israel the right to re-inherit their ancestral land, such people and nations will be judged by God.

Territorial inheritance

The second step in the Christian Zionist outlook examines the way these land promises were realized in biblical history. A principal theological motif in the Genesis–Kings narrative is "promise and fulfillment." The drama that remains with Israel is the near-crisis of its land loss. It strives to leave the captivity of Egypt, it wanders for years in the desert, and finally Israel moves toward the realization of its promise when Moses leads the tribes toward Canaan. A high point in the story of Israel's territorial inheritance is the tribal conquest under Joshua. It contrasts sharply with Israel's 40 years in the wilderness – and it is to be compared with the Egyptian sojourn. Moreover it demonstrates that God's own power is giving Israel success as the Canaanites are defeated. The book of Judges continues this drama by demonstrating that despite recurring threats to Israel's territorial integrity by neighbors, still, the inheritance of land is sacrosanct.

Perhaps the territorial motif is clearest when the tabernacle moves into the Judean hill country and ultimately a royal home is found not only for Israel's king, but for Israel's God. Despite Samuel's warnings about this arrangement, the Old Testament narrative provides this as the consummation of the promise: a gleaming temple reigns from Zion, David is enthroned, Israel's opponents are in retreat, Israel is no longer a loose confederation of tribes, but a nation, a kingdom deserving full respect from the international community. Emissaries travel to this kingdom from afar, offering gifts, paying homage, making deals, signing alliances.

In many respects, this is the station to which Christian Zionism sees Israel returning. It is not a return to the Hellenized Judaism of Roman occupation known to Jesus. It is a return to an idealized Israel that evokes stories of David, that builds an ethnic state conscious of its purity, where worship is centered on the Temple and Jewish life is concentrated within the land rather than a remote Diaspora.

It should surprise no one then that some Zionists have taken this vision as a justification for their desire to rebuild the Temple in Jerusalem and to threaten one of Islam's most holy sites, the Dome of the Rock. And it should not surprise anyone to find in Jerusalem an odd man every summer walking around outside Jerusalem's Zion Gate blowing a *shofar* (or ram's horn) and playing a harp. He thinks he looks like King David. Nor is it surprising to see Christian Zionists marching around Jerusalem in the thousands waving Israeli flags singing songs of David's glory. This is biblical reminiscence now realized in modern history.

This behavior explains why psalms that depict this era of David become the grist of worship music among Christian Zionists. Psalm 48 provides an excellent example. This is a picture of national triumph where God has settled in Jerusalem to rule and prosper his people.

> Great is the LORD and greatly to be praised in the city of our God! His holy mountain, beautiful in elevation, is the joy of all the earth, Mount Zion, in the far north, the city of the great King.
> Within her citadels God has shown himself a sure defense. For lo, the kings assembled, they came on together. As soon as they saw it, they were astounded, they were in panic, they took to flight; trembling took hold of them there, anguish as of a woman in travail. By the east wind thou didst shatter the ships of Tarshish.
> As we have heard, so have we seen in the city of the LORD of hosts, in the city of our God, which God establishes for ever. We have thought on thy steadfast love, O God, in the midst of thy temple. As thy name, O God, so thy praise reaches to the ends of the earth. Thy right hand

is filled with victory; let Mount Zion be glad! Let the daughters of Judah rejoice because of thy judgments!

Walk about Zion, go round about her, number her towers, consider well her ramparts, go through her citadels; that you may tell the next generation that this is God, our God for ever and ever. He will be our guide for ever.

(RSV)

Territorial loss and reclamation

Of course, in the Bible the golden era of the united monarchy stemming from Saul and David and Solomon did not last. Israel's national unity is fragmented, inter-tribal warfare takes on a lethal and devastating reality, Israel's neighbors exploit the disintegration and leverage their power against Jerusalem – and finally, monstrous kings from the Far East, powers Israel never imagined, begin marching across the Euphrates highway en route to Egypt. First the north, then the south are devastated within 130 years of each other. Jerusalem lies burning in the sixth century BC. But despite a crushing exile in Babylon, still, God draws his people back to their promised inheritance.

This return from the eastern exile reinforces the land cycle in the same manner as the return from the southern exile – Egypt – began it. God's promise, Israel's loss and now Israel's reclamation of land is a continuing biblical pattern.

Christian Zionists will echo the conclusion of 2 Kings and prophets such as Jeremiah. Territorial loss in biblical history reflects a failure of Israel to maintain its national mandate. However, restoration from exile and the dramatic reclamation of land demonstrate that despite the imperfections of Israel's national life, the territorial promise cannot be jeopardized. It has less to do with Israel and is chiefly centered on God who holds an unflinching commitment to his promises to the patriarchs. To deny this reclamation is to invalidate the promise and this would be the undoing of Israel's covenant life.

But the cycle of territorial loss and territorial reclamation exceeds the story of Babylon and the return under Ezra. Christian Zionists see it as well in the same manner with the Roman exile of AD 70 and 135. If the biblical cycle of loss and reclamation is correct, if exile must always be followed by restoration, if the promises to the patriarchs and their descendants are the controlling variable in Israel's history, then the return of Israel today to their ancestral land should come as no surprise. Songs of celebration found in the psalms – used to sing home the returning exiles from Babylon – now should be used to sing home those Jews returning from Krakow and Moscow and Yemen and Miami. To deny this return, to deny the significance of 1948, is to deny more than a mere political event. It is to deny the cycle of territory promised, territory lost and territory reclaimed that has been going on since Abraham's great-grandson enjoyed a forced migration to Egypt. It is a divine symmetry, a biblical program that will not change because God does not change.

A territorial eschatology

Christian Zionism's use of the Old Testament prophets is perhaps its most novel contribution. There is a surprising disregard for the prophet's ethical exhortations about the quality of Israel's national life, particularly its treatment of the "aliens and sojourners" who live among them. Instead the prophets are lifted from their original historical context where they may have warned about an Assyrian conquest or questionable alliances with Moabites or predicted a return from a Babylonian exile. Instead their warnings and predictions are given a timelessness and applied to the modern era with breathtaking confidence. Passages of comfort in Jeremiah or Ezekiel, which once reassured Israelites of life after exile, now reassure Israelis of life after 1948. Or 1967. Or 1973. Warnings about alliances with Moabites can be used to warn about alliances with modern Arab nations or peace consultations with Palestinian leadership. The prophetic message is no longer historically anchored and contextualized but instead refitted into a later application of the cycle of promise and loss and restoration.

However, what characterizes most Christian Zionists is not their careful theology of the Old Testament but the eschatology that they are eager to forge from select Old Testament texts. In this view, the cycle of promise and loss and restoration will not go on forever. In this view, there will be one more restoration – the present one – and it will culminate with the Second Coming of Jesus Christ. Suddenly we see that interest in Israel does not spring from a genuine sympathy for the Jews – though this is often claimed. Interest in Israel is not inspired by a desire to see a restoration and preservation of a biblical people to a biblical land for its own sake. Rather a commitment to the restoration of Israel springs from a desire to accelerate an eschatological crisis that will deliver the world to Armageddon and bring Christ back.

In this view, 1948 is the key which initiates the era of dramatic fulfillment which leads to something more specific: an apocalyptic Zionism. It is a theological worldview that believes fervently in the Second Coming of Christ and sees the return of Judaism to the Promised Land as the catalyst that will make it happen. Prophecies in the Old Testament that pointed to Israel's return from Babylon now are re-employed to describe Israel's return from its European exile.

Hal Lindsey popularized this view in the 1970s with his famous book *The Late Great Planet Earth.* Since then he has turned it into an evangelical industry. He has also been the most prolific while most Christian Zionists rarely explain their views with care. For Lindsey, the key to understanding the need for Israel's return is the desecration of the Temple predicted by Jesus in Mark 13. Imagine the thrill of some Christians when after the Israeli conquest of Jerusalem in 1967, Israeli Defense Force chaplain Rabbi Shlomo Goren stood next to the Dome of the Rock and blew a *shofar* and performed a religious ceremony. Such a sound had not been heard from that mountain top for almost 2,000 years. Three years later, in 1970, Hal Lindsey wrote:

> Obstacle or no obstacle, it is certain that the Temple will be rebuilt. Prophecy demands it. With the Jewish nation reborn in the land of Palestine, ancient Jerusalem once again under total Jewish control for the first time in 2600 years and talk of rebuilding the great Temple, the most important sign of Jesus Christ's soon coming is before us. It is like the key piece of the jigsaw puzzle being found. For all those who trust in Jesus Christ, it is a time of electrifying excitement.[10]

Lindsey's tone has not changed. In 2001 he wrote that "the fate of the world will be determined by an ancient feud over 35 acres of land." The Temple will be restored, Jewish worship will begin again and this will set the stage for the rapture, the antichrist, the Temple's desecration, the tribulation, Armageddon, and the Second Coming.

Today new names have become Lindsey's rivals for the Zionist stage. In 1995 fiction writers Tim LaHaye and Jerry Jenkins launched the *Left Behind* series, which soon became a 16-volume set selling over 65 million copies in multiple languages around the world. Here the authors create a fictional narrative of people who live through the final wars of humanity and witness the Second Coming of Christ.

But perhaps the most strident spokesperson for this view today is John Hagee, pastor of San Antonio's large Cornerstone Church. His most revealing books are *Jerusalem Countdown* (2005, rev. 2007) and *In Defense of Israel: The Bible's Mandate for Supporting the Jewish State* (2007), both providing specific political application to a Zionist reading of the Bible. Today *In Defense of Israel* can be found for sale in Wal-Mart stores across America and is sold throughout Europe. His defense of Israel has now become so extreme that he preaches that Jesus never claimed to be the Messiah (he will become the Messiah at his Second Coming). This means that Judaism never rejected "the Messiah" because they could not reject something that was never offered. Criticism of this view among evangelical theologians has been unrelenting.

Assessment

Numerous writers have critiqued this movement extensively and found in its bold claims to territory (linked to eschatology) an angry and dangerous synthesis of theology and politics. Engaging their writings directly is difficult because it is a populist movement fueled by preachers who use its schema evangelistically. No carefully argued theological study has come from within its own ranks. No New Testament scholar has written in its defense. Its advocacy groups, such as Christians United for Israel, and Camera, are generally run by political activists. Its books come from the pens of popular television preachers or lobbyists.[11] I have been invited to debate some of their leaders and find myself with people who have no training in theology. How can such a widespread movement in the Church be successful without a thoughtful theological undergirding?

Nevertheless, this territorial theology has many shortcomings that deserve attention. First, these Christians fail to point out the indisputable biblical motif that land promise is strictly tied to covenant fidelity. In the Old Testament this is the theme that runs from Judges to 2 Kings and the prophets. When Israel neglects the covenant, when Israel thinks that its land is now a private acquisition not linked to worship and ethics, it loses its privileges of residency. Or as Leviticus puts it ever so gently: the land will vomit you out. In the Old Testament the Babylonian armies were God's messengers of judgment.

Christian Zionists who see Israel's restoration as a resumption of biblical inheritance must square this teaching with the intentionally secular nature of Israel's national life.

Second, these Christians use the prophets to build their worldview, but they fail to hear what else the prophets had to say. Isaiah and Micah spare no words for their audiences: "Woe to you who join house to house, who add field to field, until there is room for no one but you and you are alone living in the midst of the land" (Isa. 5.8). "Woe to you…who covet fields and seize them, houses and take them away, who oppress householder and house, people and inheritance" (Mic. 2.1–3). Perhaps the story of Ahab, Jezebel, and Naboth's vineyard in 1 Kings 21 can serve as a model of God's intolerance for a calculating and politically shielded taking of land.

Christian Zionists who champion the prophetic fulfillments of modern Israel must likewise be ready to apply the prophetic ethical demands of these same writers.

Third, I would also mention the lofty national vision held up in the Old Testament for Israel's national life – a commitment to justice and fairness that has been echoed for the last two thousand years in Judaism's rich literature. The alien and sojourner is protected because Israel was an alien and sojourner in Egypt.

If Christian Zionists want to make a biblical claim for Israel's territorial promise, they need to call Israel to live by biblical standards of life.

Fourth, many have challenged the naive application to modern Israel of historic texts from Israel's ancient history. Exilic promises are often lifted from their context and offered to the twentieth century. The resumption of Israel's national life in the Middle East is an event that surprised Judaism as much as it has surprised the rest of the world. Judaism itself is in dispute over its true meaning and those Jews who critique Jewish Zionism often find themselves in partnership with Christians who critique Christian Zionism. But to refer with confidence to the events of 1948 or 1967 as divine events, as a resumption of a theological cycle, as a certain act of God, lacks a needed humility and an awareness of how millennial predictions have gone wrong in the past.

Fifth, perhaps most important, Christian Zionists fail to think Christianly about the subject of theology and the land. That is, they fail to hear what the New Testament says about these ancient debates

124

concerning the land and they use the Old Testament Scriptures without a discriminating and careful theological program. In this study we have outlined how the New Testament came to view this debate about the Holy Land. Rarely will Christian Zionists engage these perspectives.

In a recent issue of the magazine *Christian Century*, Notre Dame Old Testament scholar Gary Anderson wrote eloquently about how we ought to think about Zionism.[12] Anderson rightly identifies the inseparable link between Old Testament faith and the land and between modern Judaism and the Holy Land today. Everything about his essay is compelling, but for one not-so-insignificant detail which may be excused an Old Testament scholar. He never once looks at the question through the lens of the New Testament, never once thinks about how land has now shifted in the theological program of the Christian Church. He cites Jewish writers with approval, "Israel's providential right to the land is secure. It is the subject of a divine promise. Is the return to Zion part of God's providential design and eternal promise to his people Israel? I believe that it is." Now if you are a Jewish theologian these words may be yours, but within a Christian theological framework about land and covenant and promise, they are misplaced.

Thinking Christianly about the land

So what might be the contours of a theology of the land that is informed by the New Testament? The territoriality of the Old Testament is clear and many studies have tried to organize the many divergent emphases found in its pages. One scholar has located as many as six different models for how the Old Testament presents this theme.[13] But in the New Testament we have seen limited scholarly attention to the topic. W. D. Davies's important contribution *The Gospel and the Land* began an exploration of critical texts, but does not give us guidance for praxis in the modern world.

What the New Testament does not say

Perhaps it is helpful to begin by suggesting what views are foreign to the New Testament itself. There is no suggestion, for example, that in some manner Christians may now assume *for themselves* the land promises given to the patriarchs. Despite the clear New Testament argument that in faith followers of Christ can make a defensible claim to the legacy of Abraham, even to be called the "children of Abraham," still, the promise of that legacy – the land – is never claimed. The New Testament shows no interest in building a Christian Holy Land, no passion for constructing a kingdom in the name of Christ that might be centered at Jerusalem. We hear no calls in the New Testament that would soon become familiar to Byzantine and European armies.

This alone is remarkable. The Church was born into a Jewish world saturated with debates about territorial faith, and it chose – deliberately – not to compete as yet one more territorial religion. As we have seen, the impetus for this decision no doubt came from its Lord. The Gospels show us with keen subtlety how Jesus navigated these debates and how he dislodged his own followers from the passions that inflamed territorial movements of his day.

Neither is there any interest in the New Testament to look at the Hebrew Scriptures and Judaism and validate their territorial claims. The New Testament community did not share in the growing momentum within the first century to make the Holy Land exclusively Jewish once more. Throughout the entire century including the great war of AD 66 the followers of Jesus separated themselves from Jewish territorialism. To read the Old Testament prophetic promises into that world of Romans and Zealots might well have been seen as fantastic and perhaps naive. If the identity of the true descendants of Abraham was on the table for discussion, then simple calls for Jewish fulfillment and Christian allegiance would have sounded odd. Christian theology asked withering questions about territorial religion, especially of the sort found in Judea.

And yet, the New Testament does not dismiss the land as if it were irrelevant. As we have seen, the Gospels do not talk about the revelation of Christ without referring to the place where it happened. Location is valuable because history is important. In the New Testament the incarnation is a genuine embrace of human life with all of its particularities. And what emerges is the wedding of theology and history which together form the nexus of how Christians begin to think about their world and Christ. Davies remarks,

The emergence of the gospels – kerygmatic as they might be – witnesses to a historical and, therefore, geographic concern in the tradition, which retains for the *realia* their full physical significance. Jesus belonged not only to time but to space; and the space and the spaces which he occupied took on significance, so that the *realia* of Judaism continued as the *realia* in Christianity. History in the tradition demanded geography.[14]

Thus a commitment to incarnational theology demands a commitment to *place* as having significance. The faith of the Church was not Gnostic at this very point. Revelation did not occur outside of human history but within it. The Holy Land continued to be holy because it was the locale of divine revelation.

In sum, the New Testament is asking a different set of questions, and once they are heard, the older questions of territorial theologies become obsolete. The New Testament is not prone to ask, "Who owns the land?" The New Testament wonders first about God's relation to the land and how Christ in entering the land changed it. Jesus' views here become instructive. In the great story of the vineyard – which as we learned is the Land of Promise – Jesus up-ends the expectation that the vineyard can be possessed. God is the sole owner (in the synoptic story) and those tenants – yes, they are tenants only – must realize that the true owner may arrive and end their tenure. Then in John 15 the vineyard motif is spun in another direction. Christ alone is attached to "the land" and the final question is not whether we are planted in the land, whether we can take holy land for ourselves, but whether we are attached to him. *Ownership of the land is not a Christian question.* The New Testament instead asks if we know the landowner himself or, in a different framework, whether the land owns us. To plot, grasp, and take as if the land were a commodity and we own a spiritual mandate to do so is not a reflex known in the New Testament.

Contours of a New Testament theology of the land

So what does the New Testament say that bears relevance for a modern conversation about the land, particularly in volatile conflicts like those in the Middle East?

Historic remembrance

Brueggemann distinguishes between what he calls "space" and "place." Space "means an arena of freedom" where there is no accountability, there is emptiness, and perhaps neutrality. We can control space, make it a commodity, have it serve our purposes. But place is a different matter. "Place is a space that has historical meanings, where some things have happened that are now remembered and that provide continuity and identity across the generations."[15] In this sense a place can make claims on us, demand that we conform to what it preserves, and require humility and care.

In biblical theology, the land is never empty space which an owner can claim or use on his own. The land is a place in which God has moved; where he has revealed himself, calling his people to make vows, giving them roots in their spiritual history. The great temptation is for God's people to treat the Holy Land as space, as something to be possessed, as blank land, as something owned that makes no claim on its resident. The great temptation has always been to grasp the land and to commoditize it as a political holding.

Because of the great deeds of salvation found in the land, Christians have wisely cultivated a reflex of veneration and respect for this land. This is not to say that this land is superior to other lands around the world; but this land has value because of the story that it tells. It tells of a concrete series of events contextualized in the cultures of this land. And all other lands can look to it to discover something of their own salvation and hope.

This does not mean that the Holy Land conveys spiritual promises which are unavailable elsewhere. Baptism in the Jordan is not more efficacious than baptism in Paris or Boston. Sand carried home in plastic vials from Jericho will not have healing properties *because* it is Holy Land sand. Nevertheless this land is a land which when met with faith has the power to speak its story. Pilgrimage is a good thing, not so we can collect spiritual trinkets or magical souvenirs. But so that we can revisit the events of history that save us and renew what God has said and done in our behalf. The Church of the Holy Sepulcher is sacred because of the sobering events that occurred within its walls. But to claim to possess it by right, to presume to own it and to think that it will bring benefit is misguided. It is to heed the advice of Ahab and Jezebel.

Incarnation and land

The New Testament church did not reach back into the Old Testament to find a theological place for the land. It looked to Christ. For them, the land did not simply become a metaphor for some spiritual exercise. To say that the New Testament spiritualizes the land in this respect misses the mark (*contra* Davies). Rather the New Testament relocates the properties of the Holy Land and discovers them in Christ himself. "The New Testament finds holy space wherever Christ has been."[16] Thus the most sacred of all places, the Temple, is found in Christ. And so he too offers the "place" of residence for Christians who yearn for a "better country."

This means that the New Testament is free to deflect interest away from the land *as land*. Inasmuch as Christ lives with and indwells his community, so they find their locale for life in relationship with him. As the tribes of Israel sought a place in Canaan so Christians have found a place with Christ. This means that for a Christian to pursue the Holy Land as an object of religious desire is to be truly mistaken about what the New Testament claims. The New Testament holds deep respect for the land while pressing believers to go into every land; it promises that Christ will be with them to the ends of the earth (Matthew 28; Acts 1). Now the claim of the children of Abraham is for the whole world (Romans 4).

Perhaps the most incisive theological explanation of this theme belongs to Karl Barth.[17] Because of what he had seen in two wars culminating in the destruction of European Jewish life, Barth rightly supported the founding of Israel in 1948 as a moral and political necessity. However, in his *Dogmatics* he carefully outlined why any territorial theology was a profound error for Christians. After surveying the evidence of the New Testament, he concluded that if Christians pursued an interest in "Holy Land" it would be a theological regression of the first order. A "relapse into Judaism,"[18] Barth said. There is one reason for his view:

> There does not exist any more a holy mountain or a holy city or holy land which can be marked on a map. The reason is not that God's holiness in space has suddenly become unworthy of Him or has changed into a heathen ubiquity. The reason is that all prophecy is now fulfilled in Jesus, and God's holiness in space, like all God's holiness, is now called and is Jesus of Nazareth.[19]

Therefore the New Testament locates in Christ all of the expectations once held for "Sinai and Zion, Bethel and Jerusalem." For a Christian to return to Jewish territoriality is to deny fundamentally what has transpired in the incarnation. It is to deflect appropriate devotion to the new place where God has appeared in residence, namely, in his Son. This explains why the New Testament applies to the person of Christ religious language formerly devoted to the Holy Land or the Temple. He is the new spatiality, the new locale where God may be met.

Landless yet landed

This disconnection–connection to the land invites a paradox unique to those who claim to be followers of Christ. They are connected to the land inasmuch as the events of Christ's life speak to us from its many biblical sites. Or as Fr Bargil Pixner, a Benedictine Monk at the Dormition Abbey in Jerusalem, puts it: the land is for Christians a "Fifth Gospel," telling us the gospel story by recording in real place and time the events of Jesus' life.[20] And yet while Pixner would lead us on memorable walks into the Holy Land, still, as a good theologian he would remind us that God does not dwell here in a manner that is uniquely different from his dwelling in other lands.

Christians do live in other "lands" and these also require some interpretation *as land*. The problem with losing a sense of holy land is that theology experiences a loss of holy space and generally reverts to promoting the general "presence" or ubiquity of God in all places. *God is everywhere but ultimately cannot be located anywhere.* But while this has some merit – particularly as it brings value and significance to all lands equally – it misses something significant again from the New Testament. If Christ who is the locus of divine presence has ascended to the right hand of God, the gift of the Spirit to the Church now suggests that something else is afoot in the world. It is no accident that the New Testament refers to the Church as *the body of Christ*. The Church is a secondary place where God can once again meet the world; it is a space rendered with divinely given obligations and privileges to do what Christ has done in the world.

Thus the New Testament can freely and extravagantly speak of the Church as a temple of the living God, a place where in the Spirit the Father and the Son choose now to take up a dwelling (John 14.23; 1 Pet. 2.9). The New Testament therefore brings an ecclesial alternative to the problem of Holy Land. Christians in other lands, lands deeply valued by God, bring with them the possibility of bearing the reality of Christ to these places. Which explains the fundamental basis of Christian mission. This is a divinely appointed task to bring that which the Temple and the land once held – the presence of God – into the nations of the world.

When Christian theology serves at the behest of political or historical forces in any generation – be it ancient crusades, religiously fueled nationalism, or the call of Christian Zionists – it loses its supreme mission in the world. Such theologies immediately neglect the centrality of what has transpired in Christ, they compete with the ideologies of the world that strive for power and control, and finally they become unfaithful to their Lord. The drama and success of the New Testament message is that it was able to speak a prophetic word in a world little different from our own. Amidst calls to reclaim holy land, to reconquer territory in the name of God, to assume religious privileges for one tribe and not another, the New Testament says: No. Jesus called for a faithfulness that abandoned such things, that envisioned a different era, a different kingdom, where old territorial claims backed by religious privilege were no more.

Notes

Introduction: land, place, and religion

1 See Pappe, I., *The Ethnic Cleansing of Palestine* (Oxford: Oneworld, 2007).

2 Boyarin, D., *A Radical Jew: Paul and the Politics of Identity* (Berkeley: University of California Press, 1994), 252.

1 The biblical heritage

1 Brueggemann, W., *The Land: Place as Gift, Promise and Challenge in Biblical Faith*, 2nd edn (Minneapolis: Fortress, 2002), 3.

2 Davies, W. D., *The Gospel and the Land* (Berkeley: University of California Press, 1974). See also his *The Territorial Dimension of Judaism* (Minneapolis: Fortress, 1982).

3 Davies, *Territorial Dimension*, 19.

4 Cited in Davies, *The Gospel and the Land*, 56.

5 Today, Beit She'arim and the countless tombs of Diaspora Jews can be visited at the site, revered by Jews worldwide.

2 Diaspora Judaism and the land

1 Panayotov, A., "The Jews in the Balkan Provinces of the Roman Empire: The Evidence from the Territory of Bulgaria," in Barclay, J. M. G., ed., *Negotiating Diaspora: Jewish Strategies in the Roman Empire* (London: T&T Clark, 2004), 38–65.

2 Evans, C., and Trebilco, P. R., "Diaspora Judaism," in Evans, C., and Porter, S., *Dictionary of New Testament Backgrounds* (Downers Grove: IVP, 2000), 285.

3 For their location, Schürer, E., with Vermes, G., Millar, F., and Goodman, M., eds, *The History of the Jewish People in the Age of Jesus Christ*, vol. 3.1 (Edinburgh: T&T Clark, 1986), 8–9.

4 These frescoes are now on display in the National Archaeological Museum, Damascus, Syria.

5 Schürer, *History of the Jewish People*, 3.1.21–2.

6 Barclay, J. M. G., *Jews in the Mediterranean Diaspora from Alexander to Trajan (323 BCE–117 CE)* (Edinburgh: T&T Clark, 1996).

7 Cited in Schürer, *History of the Jewish People*, 3.1.141 and 2.448 n. 102.

8 Schürer, *History of the Jewish People*, 3.1.124–5, 147–9.
9 Schürer, *History of the Jewish People*, 3.1.138.
10 Cited in Evans, C., and Trebilco, P. R., "Diaspora Judaism," in Evans, C., and Porter, S., *Dictionary of New Testament Backgrounds* (Downers Grove: IVP, 2000), 293–4.
11 Amaru, B. H., "Land Theology in Philo and Josephus," in Hoffman, L. A., ed., *The Land of Israel, Jewish Perspectives* (Notre Dame: University of Notre Dame Press, 1986), 65–91.
12 Amaru, "Land Theology in Philo and Josephus," 86.
13 Amaru, "Land Theology in Philo and Josephus," 86.

3 Jesus and the land

1 Brandon, S. G. F., *Jesus and the Zealots: A Study of the Political Factor in Primitive Christianity* (Manchester: Manchester University Press, 1967).
2 Crossan, John Dominic, *The Historical Jesus: The Life of a Mediterranean Jewish Peasant* (New York: HarperOne; Edinburgh: T&T Clark, 1991).
3 Wright, N. T., *Jesus and the Victory of God* (Minneapolis: Fortress; London: SPCK, 1997), 83–91; see also Horbury, W., "Christ as Brigand in Ancient Anti-Christian Polemic," in Bammel, E., and Moule, C. F. D., eds, *Jesus and the Politics of His Day* (Cambridge: Cambridge University Press, 1984), 183–95.
4 See the classic treatment of Stauffer, E., "Christ and the Story of the Tribute Money," in *Christ and the Caesars* (English Translation; London: SCM Press, 1955).
5 See the remarks of Marchadour, A., and Neuhaus, D., *The Land, the Bible, and History* (New York: Fordham University Press, 2007), 61–77.
6 Schnabel, E., *Mission in the New Testament* (Downers Grove: IVP, 2004), 327–82. Schnabel rejects the critical consensus and argues that Jesus was indeed convinced that mission must go beyond the confines of traditional Judea.
7 See France, R. T., *The Gospel of Matthew* (Grand Rapids: Eerdmans, 2007), 381.
8 Resseguie, J., *Spiritual Landscape: Images of the Spiritual Life in the Gospel of Luke* (Peabody: Hendricksen, 2004).
9 France, *The Gospel of Matthew*, 166.
10 Hagner, D., *Matthew 1–13*, Word Biblical Commentary, 33A (Grand Rapids: Word, 1993), 92.
11 Herrmann, J., *kleros, Theological Dictionary of the New Testament* (Grand Rapids: Eerdmans, 1964), 3.759–61.
12 For some interpreters, the term *ge* should remain "earth" and refer to the Jewish hope of a regenerated world. See Rom. 4.13.

13 Brueggemann, W., *The Land: Place as Gift, Promise and Challenge in Biblical Faith*, 2nd edn (Minneapolis: Fortress, 2002), 164.

14 Brueggemann, *The Land*, 162.

15 So Davies, W. D., *The Gospel and the Land* (Berkeley: University of California Press, 1974), 355.

16 For the many ways the fig served as a Jewish symbol, see Snodgrass, K., *Stories with Intent: A Comprehensive Guide to the Parables of Jesus* (Grand Rapids: Eerdmans, 2008), 259–60.

17 Marshall, I. H., *The Gospel of Luke: A Commentary on the Greek Text* (Grand Rapids: Eerdmans; Exeter: Paternoster, 1978), 555.

18 Snodgrass, *Stories with Intent*, 256–7, provides examples from early Judaism, Greco-Roman writings, early Christian apocrypha, and later Jewish writings.

19 For a review of discussion and literature, see Snodgrass, *Stories with Intent*, 276–99, and his earlier, "Recent Research on the Parable of the Wicked Tenants: An Assessment," *Bulletin for Biblical Research* 8 (1998), 187–215.

20 These thematic connections and their application to Matthew 19 are outlined in Davies, *The Gospel and the Land*, 363ff. See also Wright, *Jesus and the Victory of God*, 320–68.

21 Brueggemann, *The Land*, 164.

22 Brueggemann, *The Land*, 161.

4 The Fourth Gospel and the Land

1 Dodd, C. H., *Historical Tradition in the Fourth Gospel* (Cambridge: Cambridge University Press, 1963); Anderson, P. N., "Aspects of Historicity in the Gospel of John: Implications for Investigations of Jesus and Archaeology," in Charlesworth, J., ed., *Jesus and Archaeology* (Grand Rapids: Eerdmans, 2006), 587–618.

2 Burge, G., *Interpreting the Gospel of John* (Grand Rapids: Baker, 1992); Blomberg, C., *The Historical Reliability of John's Gospel* (Leicester: Apollos; Downers Grove: IVP, 2001); Ashton, J., *Understanding the Fourth Gospel*, 2nd edn (Oxford: Oxford University Press, 2007).

3 For a summary of John and recent archaeology, see von Wahlde, U., "Archaeology and John's Gospel," in Charlesworth, J., ed., *Jesus and Archaeology* (Grand Rapids: Eerdmans, 2006), 523–86.

4 The original announcement of archaeologist Eli Shukrun appeared in the *Jerusalem Post*, June 10, 2004, p. 5. See also Shanks, H., "The Siloam Pool: Where Jesus Cured the Blind Man," *Biblical Archaeology Review* 31.5 (2005), 16–23; von Wahlde, U., "The Pool of Siloam: The Importance of the New Discoveries for Our Understanding of Ritual Immersion in Late Second Temple Judaism and the Gospel of John," in Anderson, P., Just, F., and Thatcher, T., *John, Jesus, and History*,

vol. 2, *Aspects of Historicity in the Fourth Gospel* (Atlanta: SBL, 2009), 155–74.

5 Davies, W. D., *The Gospel and the Land* (Berkeley: University of California Press, 1974), 289.

6 Robinson, J. A. T., *The Priority of John* (London: SCM Press, 1985), 52, citing C. H. H. Scobie (without reference).

7 Robinson, *The Priority of John*, 67.

8 Most famously presented by Brown, R. E., *The Community of the Beloved Disciple* (New York: Paulist Press; London: Geoffrey Chapman, 1979) and Martyn, J. L., *History and Theology in the Fourth Gospel*, 2nd edn (Nashville: Abingdon, 1979).

9 See the contrary view of Kerr, A. R., *The Temple of Jesus' Body: The Temple Theme in the Gospel of John*, Journal for the Study of the New Testament Suppl. Series 220 (Sheffield: Sheffield Academic Press, 2002), 136–66.

10 Köstenberger, A., "Destruction of the Temple and the Composition of the Fourth Gospel," in Lierman, J., ed., *Challenging Perspectives on the Gospel of John* (Tübingen: Siebeck, 2006), 97–103.

11 McKelvey, R. J., *The New Temple: The Church in the New Testament* (Oxford: Oxford University Press, 1969); Walker, P. W. L., *Jesus and the Holy City. New Testament Perspectives on Jerusalem* (Grand Rapids: Eerdmans, 1996); Beale, G., *The Temple and the Church's Mission: A Biblical Theology of the Temple* (Downers Grove: IVP, 2004); Gray, T., *The Temple in the Gospel of Mark: A Study in Its Narrative Role*, Wissenschaftliche Untersuchungen Zum Neuen Testament, 2 Reihe (Tübingen: Mohr Siebeck, 2008; reprinted, Grand Rapids: Baker, 2010).

12 See Nereparampil, L., *Destroy this Temple: An Exegetico-Theological Study of Jesus's Temple-Logion in Jn 2.19* (Bangalore: Dharmaram College, 1978).

13 Davies, *The Gospel and the Land*, 294.

14 Davies, *The Gospel and the Land*, 295.

15 McCaffrey, J., *The House with Many Rooms: The Temple Theme of Jn 14, 2–3* (Rome: Biblical Institute Press, 1988).

16 Barrett, C. K., *The Gospel According to St. John*, 2nd edn (London: SPCK, 1978), 393.

17 Behm's article on *ampelos*, in *Theological Dictionary of the New Testament* (Grand Rapids: Eerdmans, 1964), 1.342f.; Brown, R. A., *The Gospel According to John* (New York: Doubleday, 1970), 2.669; Johnston, G., "The Allegory of the Vine," *Canadian Journal of Theology* 3 (1957), 150–8; and Rosscup, J., *Abiding in Christ: Studies in John 15* (Grand Rapids: Zondervan, 1973).

18 Jaubert, A., "L'image de la Vigne (Jean 15)," in Christ, F., ed., *Oikonomia: Heilsgeschichte als Thema der Theologie: O. Cullmann zum 65 Geburtstag gewidmet* (Hamburg: Reich, 1957), 93–9.

19 Bultmann, R., *The Gospel of John* (English Translation; Oxford: Blackwell; Philadelphia: Westminster, 1971), 529–32, gives ample evidence for the use of this metaphor. Cf. Behm, in *Theological Dictionary of the New Testament*, 1.342–3.

5 The book of Acts and the land

1 Scott, J. M., "Luke's Geographical Horizon," in Gill, D. W. J., and Gempf, C., eds, *The Book of Acts in Its First Century Setting*, vol. 2: *Greco-Roman Setting* (Grand Rapids: Eerdmans; Carlisle: Paternoster, 1994), 483–544.

2 Wright, C., "A Christian Approach to Old Testament Prophecy," in Walker, P. W. L., ed., *Jerusalem Past and Present in the Purposes of God* (Cambridge: Tyndale, 1992), 1–19.

3 Wright, N. T., "Jerusalem in the New Testament," in Walker, P. W. L., ed., *Jerusalem Past and Present in the Purposes of God* (Cambridge: Tyndale, 1992), 63.

4 Walker, P. W. L., *Jesus and the Holy City* (Grand Rapids: Eerdmans, 1996), 292.

5 Davies, W. D., *The Gospel and the Land* (Berkeley: University of California Press, 1974), 266.

6 Bruce, F. F., *The Acts of the Apostles: Greek Text with Introduction and Commentary*, 3rd edn (Leicester: Apollos; Grand Rapids: Eerdmans, 1990), 188.

7 Köster, H., "*topos*," in *Theological Dictionary of the New Testament* (Grand Rapids: Eerdmans, 1964), 8.193.

8 Palmer, D. W., "Acts and the Ancient Historical Monograph," in Winter, B., and Clarke, A. D., eds, *The Book of Acts in Its First Century Setting*, vol. 1: *Ancient Literary Setting* (Grand Rapids: Eerdmans; Carlisle: Paternoster, 1993), 1–30. Cf. Rosner, B. S., "Acts and Biblical History," in Winter, B., and Clarke, A. D. eds, *The Book of Acts in Its First Century Setting*, vol. 1: *Ancient Literary Setting* (Grand Rapids: Eerdmans; Carlisle: Paternoster, 1993), 65–82.

9 Simon, M., *St. Stephen and the Hellenists in the Primitive Church* (London: Longmans, 1958), 44.

10 Davies, *The Gospel and the Land*, 270.

11 Murphy-O'Connor, J., *Paul: A Critical Life* (Oxford: Clarendon, 1996), 32–70.

12 Dahl, N., "The Story of Abraham in Luke–Acts," in Keck, L., and Martyn, J. L., eds, *Studies in Luke–Acts* (London: SPCK, 1953), 153.

13 Davies, *The Gospel and the Land*, 271.

14 Manson, W., *The Epistle to the Hebrews* (London: Hodder & Stoughton, 1951), 35; cited in Davies, *The Gospel and the Land*, 272.

6 Paul and the promises to Abraham

1 Walker, P. W. L., *Jesus and the Holy City* (Grand Rapids: Eerdmans, 1996), 114–16.

2 Davies, W. D., *The Gospel and the Land* (Berkeley: University of California Press, 1974), 166–8.

3 Wright, N. T., "Jerusalem in the New Testament," in Walker, P. W. L., ed., *Jerusalem Past and Present in the Purposes of God* (Cambridge: Tyndale, 1992), 70; cited in Walker, *Jesus and the Holy City*, 120.

4 Walker, *Jesus and the Holy City*, 121.

5 Davies, *The Gospel and the Land*, 168; Calvert, N., "Traditions of Abraham in Middle Jewish Literature: Implications for the Interpretation of Paul's Epistles to the Galatians and the Romans," unpublished Ph.D. dissertation, University of Sheffield, 1993.

6 Davies, *The Gospel and the Land*, 177; Barrett, C. K., *From First Adam to Last: A Study in Pauline Theology* (London: Black; New York: Scribners, 1962), 31; cf. Käsemann, E., "The Faith of Abraham in Romans 4," in *Perspectives on Paul* (London: SCM Press; Philadelphia: Fortress, 1971), 86.

7 Nanos, M. D., *The Irony of Galatians: Paul's Letter in First Century Context* (Minneapolis: Fortress, 2002).

8 Boyarin, D., *A Radical Jew: Paul and the Politics of Identity* (Berkeley: University of California Press, 1997).

9 Boyarin, *A Radical Jew*, 106.

10 Dunn, J. D. G., *The Theology of Paul the Apostle* (Edinburgh: T&T Clark; Grand Rapids: Eerdmans, 1998), 382.

11 Davies, *The Gospel and the Land*, 176.

12 Wright, N. T., *The Climax of the Covenant: Christ and the Law in Pauline Theology* (Edinburgh: T&T Clark; Minneapolis: Fortress, 1992), 162–8; also Boyarin, *A Radical Jew*, 145 n. 19, who notes that in Aramaic the root meaning of seed is the regular word for family.

13 Bruce, F. F., *The Epistle to the Galatians: A Commentary on the Greek Text* (Exeter: Paternoster; Grand Rapids: Eerdmans, 1982), 172–3; Daube, D., "The Interpretation of the Generic Singular," in Daube, D., *The New Testament and Rabbinic Judaism* (London: Athlone, 1956), 438–44. Bruce notes the use of Heb. *zera'* (seed) in the Mishnah, *Shab.* 9.2 and elsewhere; and the use of *dam* (blood) in *Genesis Rabbah* 22.9.

14 Dunn, J. D. G., *The Epistle to the Galatians* (London: Black, 1993), 184.

15 Here I am thinking about dispensational interpreters who wish to preserve the ongoing efficacy of the Abrahamic covenant and find themselves turning Paul's teaching in this chapter on its head.

16 Wright, N. T., *Paul: A Fresh Perspective* (London: SPCK; Minneapolis: Fortress, 2005), 113–14. See also his *The Climax of the Covenant*, 157–74.

17 Some refer to this as an allegory. On the important difference, see Fung, R. Y., *The Epistle to the Galatians* (Grand Rapids: Eerdmans, 1988), 217–20.

18 Fung, *The Epistle to the Galatians*, 311 n. 67; also Wright, *Paul: A Fresh Perspective*, 114.

19 Dunn, *The Epistle to the Galatians*, 344.

20 Fitzmyer, J., *Romans* (New York: Doubleday, 1993), 384.

21 Cited in Wright, N. T., *The New Testament and the People of God* (London: SPCK; Minneapolis: Fortress, 1993), 251.

22 Wright, *The New Testament and the People of God*, 263.

23 Barrett, C. K., *From First Adam to Last* (London: Black, 1962), 34.

24 Wright, N. T., "Jerusalem in the New Testament," 67.

25 Robertson, O. P., "A New Covenant Perspective on the Land," in Johnston, P., and Walker, P., eds, *The Land of Promise* (Downers Grove: IVP, 2000), 135.

26 Schnabel, E., *Mission in the New Testament* (Downers Grove: IVP, 2004), 1316–20.

27 Walker, *Jesus and the Holy City*, 127.

28 The theological proposal that a Gentile Church has now replaced the Jewish people in the economy of God. The term comes from the English, supersede, or replace, and it suggests that in some manner, God's covenant relationship with Judaism (outside Christ) has come to an end. For most, this view has inspired a history of Christian anti-Semitism. See Diprose, R. E., ed., *Israel and the Church: The Origins and Effects of Replacement Theology* (Rome: Istituto Biblico Evangelico, 2000, 2004); and Blaising, C., and Bock, D. L., *Dispensationalism, Israel and the Church: The Search for Definition* (Grand Rapids: Zondervan, 1992).

29 Wright, *Paul: A Fresh Perspective*, 126.

7 Developments beyond Paul

1 Wright, N. T., *Surprised by Hope: Rethinking Heaven, the Resurrection, and the Mission of the Church* (New York: Harper, 2008) warns against Western Christian tendencies to promote a disembodied heavenly life that is escapist.

2 Walker, P. W. L., *Jesus and the Holy City* (Grand Rapids: Eerdmans, 1996), 201–34.

3 Walker, *Jesus and the Holy City*, 210.

4 Johnson, W. G., "The Pilgrimage: A Motif in the Book of Hebrews," *Journal of Biblical Literature* 97 (1978), 239–51.

5 Walker, *Jesus and the Holy City*, 213.

6 For examples, see Ford, J. M., *Revelation* (New York: Doubleday, 1975), 3–26.

7 Much of this summary draws significantly from Mounce, R., *The Book of Revelation* (Grand Rapids: Eerdmans, 1977), 39–44; and Walker, *Jesus and the Holy City*, 235–8.

8 A recent treatment of Revelation that debates with futurists using an idealist/preterist methodology is Barbara Rossing's *The Rapture Exposed: The Message of Hope in the Book of Revelation* (New York: Basic Books, 2005).

9 Ford, J. M., *Revelation*, 215–17.

10 Walker, *Jesus and the Holy City*, 249.

8 Land, theology, and the Church

1 Habel, N., *The Land is Mine: Six Biblical Land Ideologies* (Minneapolis: Fortress, 1995), 2.

2 Habel, *The Land is Mine*, 2.

3 Online at <http://www.new-life.net/israel.htm>

4 Burge, G. M., *Whose Land? Whose Promise? What Christians Are Not Being Told About Israel and the Palestinians* (Cleveland: Pilgrim; London: Paternoster, 2003).

5 New York: H. Holt/Times Books, 2006. Also among Jewish critics see Ben-Ami, Shlomo, *Scars of War, Wounds of Peace: The Israeli–Arab Tragedy* (Oxford: Oxford University Press, 2006) and Boyarin, D., *A Radical Jew: Paul and the Politics of Identity* (Berkeley: University of California Press, 1994), 251–9, who sees modern Israel as linked not to rabbinic commitments to land but to a secular colonialism born in Europe. A European analysis is found in Veracini, Lorenzo, *Israel and Settler Society* (London: Pluto Press, 2006); and from the Arab side, Karmi, Ghada, *Married to Another Man* (London: Pluto Press, 2007).

6 Sizer, S., *Christian Zionism: Road-Map to Armageddon* (Downers Grove and Nottingham: Inter-Varsity, 2005). Also see *Zion's Christian Soldiers?: The Bible, Israel and the Church* (Downers Grove and Nottingham: Inter-Varsity, 2007).

7 Weber, T., *On the Road to Armageddon: How Evangelicals Became Israel's Best Friend* (Grand Rapids: Baker Academic, 2005).

8 Smith, Robert O., "Christian Zionism: It Challenges Our Lutheran Commitments," *The Lutheran* 164 (June 2009), 1. In this issue the ELCA devoted an entire issue to Christian Zionism. Online at: <http://www.thelutheran.org/article/issue.cfm?issue=164>

9 Smith, "Christian Zionism," *The Lutheran* 164 (June 2009), 1.

10 Lindsey, H., *The Late Great Planet Earth* (Grand Rapids: Zondervan, 1970), 56–8. Today this book is still available and was revised in its 25th printing in a new 1998 edition.

11 Brog, D., *Standing with Israel: Why Christians Support the Jewish State* (Washington: Frontline, 2006). Brog is a Jewish attorney who works in Washington, DC. He represents the close link between Israeli lobbyists and Christian Zionists in Washington. John Hagee wrote the foreword to the present book.

12 Anderson, G., "Does the Promise Still Hold? Israel and the Land. An Essay and Responses," *Christian Century* (January 13, 2009); a previous form of the same essay appeared in the Roman Catholic journal *First Things: A Monthly Journal of Religion and Public Life* 152 (April 2005).

13 Habel, *The Land is Mine: Six Biblical Land Ideologies*.

14 Davies, W. D., *The Gospel and the Land* (Berkeley: University of California Press, 1974), 366.

15 Brueggemann, W., *The Land: Place as Gift, Promise and Challenge in Biblical Faith*, 2nd edn (Minneapolis: Fortress, 2002), 4.

16 Davies, *The Gospel and the Land*, 366.

17 Barth, K., *Church Dogmatics: The Doctrine of God*, II.1 (English Translation: Edinburgh: T&T Clark, 1957), 480–3. This passage was shown to me by theologian and Barth scholar Dr David Lauber. See also, Lilburne, G. R., "The Christification of Holy Space: Incarnation and the Land," in *A Sense of Place: A Christian Theology of the Land* (Nashville: Abingdon, 1989), 89–110.

18 Barth, *Church Dogmatics* II.1, 482.

19 Barth, *Church Dogmatics* II.1, 482.

20 Pixner, B., *With Jesus Through Galilee: According to the Fifth Gospel* (Jerusalem: Chorazin, 1992).

Further reading

There have been a limited number of treatments of the land motif in the Bible. Many work directly on the problem of land conflict in Israel–Palestine and then provide theological reflection as a feature of the ethical discussion. Others – Jewish and Palestinian writers – inevitably express their own narratives within the struggle. This is a brief, annotated list of the most helpful resources that will continue the discussion.

Ateek, Naim, *Justice and Only Justice: A Palestinian Theology of Liberation* (Maryknoll: Orbis, 1989)
> Perhaps the only Palestinian "liberation theologian" today, Ateek is an Anglican priest who serves in Jerusalem leading his justice ministry called Sabeel.

Ateek, Naim, *A Palestinian Christian Cry for Reconciliation* (Maryknoll: Orbis, 2008)
> The long-awaited sequel to Ateek's 1989 contribution here provides a formula for how peace might be realized and how theological ethics might be applied in land disputes.

Barclay, J. M. G., ed., *Negotiating Diaspora: Jewish Strategies in the Roman Empire* (London: T&T Clark, 2004)
> A scholarly study of how Jewish life in the Hellenistic Diaspora was forced to reinterpret land and location as a theological and pragmatic category.

Boyarin, D., *A Radical Jew: Paul and the Politics of Identity* (Berkeley: University of California Press, 1994)
> A thorough study of Paul's continuity and discontinuity with his native Judaism and, for this subject, how Paul dealt with the covenant promises (the land promises) of Israel.

Brueggemann, W., *The Land: Place as Gift, Promise and Challenge in Biblical Faith*, 2nd edn (Minneapolis: Fortress, 2002)
> Perhaps the premier treatment of the land motif in the Old Testament. Limited attention to New Testament texts.

Burge, G. M., *Whose Land? Whose Promise? What Christians are Not Being Told about Israel and the Palestinians* (Cleveland: Pilgrim; London: Paternoster, 2003)
> An attempt to ask how the biblical land promises should be understood by Christians in the midst of the Israeli–Palestinian conflict.

Davies, W. D., *The Gospel and the Land* (Berkeley: University of California Press, 1974)

The first significant technical treatment of the land motif in the New Testament. Although hampered with a dated form-critical view of the Gospels, still the most important study of the major texts in print.

Davies, W. D., *The Territorial Dimension of Judaism* (Minneapolis: Fortress, 1982)

A concise summary of Davies's 1974 study now with contemporary application. Multiple scholars provide concluding essays on the meaning of land and theology in light of the 1967 war.

Ellis, Mark, *Toward a Jewish Theology of Liberation* (Waco: Baylor University Press, 2004)

One of the few Jewish authors to write a liberation theology for Jews – while at the same time applying his themes to modern Israel and problems of justice there.

Habel, N., *The Land is Mine: Six Biblical Land Ideologies* (Minneapolis: Fortress, 1995)

A technical study of land motifs in the Hebrew Scriptures. Habel shows how a singular view of the land is unattainable and multiple strands of thought can be found.

House, H.W., ed., *Israel: The Land and the People: An Evangelical Affirmation of God's Promises* (Grand Rapids: Kregel, 1998)

An evangelical defense of the land promises for modern Israel often used by Christian Zionists to buttress modern conservative political theologies.

Johnston, P., and Walker, P., eds, *The Land of Promise* (Downers Grove: IVP, 2000)

A conservative Christian reappraisal of the land promises and their application in modern Israel–Palestine. An opposite view from House (see above).

Loden, L., Walker, P., and Wood, M., *The Bible and the Land: An Encounter* (Jerusalem: Musalaha, 2000)

An important collection of essays by Western, Messianic, and Palestinian theologians assessing land theology and ethical applications in Israel–Palestine.

Sizer, S., *Zion's Christian Soldiers? The Bible, Israel and the Church* (Downers Grove and Nottingham: Inter-Varsity Press, 2007)

An important study of how Christian Zionists have used land theology in their political ambitions in Israel–Palestine.

Walker, P. W. L., ed., *Jerusalem Past and Present in the Purposes of God* (Cambridge: Tyndale, 1992)

A collection of essays studying the theological place of Jerusalem in the promises of God and the realization of those promises today in Israel–Palestine.

Walker, P. W. L., *Jesus and the Holy City: New Testament Perspectives on Jerusalem* (Grand Rapids: Eerdmans, 1996)
An essential study of how Jerusalem (as the premier expression of promised land) is treated in the New Testament.

Weber, Timothy, *On the Road to Armageddon: How Evangelicals Became Israel's Best Friend* (Grand Rapids: Baker, 2004)
An historian surveys the history of evangelical theology regarding Israel and the Promised Land and how it has been used in Christian Zionism.

The Israel–Palestine conflict

The conflict in Israel–Palestine is about land. And yet, how do we integrate our theological conclusions about "holy land" with modern realities? Understanding the competing voices in this political struggle is necessary, but the number of books in this area is legion. This is a short list of resources I have found most interesting from both sides of the debate. Some are personal narratives that provide insight into the human experience there, others are political analyses.

Ben-Ami, Shlomo, *Scars of War, Wounds of Peace: The Israeli–Arab Tragedy* (Oxford: Oxford University Press, 2006)
An Israeli historian takes a critical but balanced look at Israel's treatment of the Arabs throughout the twentieth century.

Carter, Jimmy, *Palestine: Peace Not Apartheid* (New York: Simon & Schuster, 2006)
A former president with long experience in Israel–Palestine negotiations reflects on the problems and the solutions in this very controversial book.

Chacour, E., *Blood Brothers*, expanded edition (Grand Rapids: Chosen Books, 2003)
A Christian priest in Galilee tells his childhood story of loss and deportation from Galilee in 1948. This is often a readable "first book" for people opening this topic.

Dunsky, Marda, *Pens and Swords: How the American Mainstream Media Report the Israeli–Palestinian Conflict* (New York: Columbia University Press, 2008)
A former Arab affairs editor for the *Jerusalem Post*, Dunsky analyzes as an Israeli how the American media interprets the Israeli–Arab conflicts.

Goldberg, J., *Prisoners: A Muslim and a Jew Across the Middle East Divide* (New York: Knopf, 2006)
An American Jew from New York goes to Israel to join the army, is assigned as a prison guard (Ketzriot prison camp) and befriends an Arab.

Further reading

Hass, Amira, *Drinking the Sea at Gaza* (New York: Holt/Owl Books, 2000)
A Jewish journalist describes the difficulties of her life and work in Gaza.

Khalidi, Rashid, *The Iron Cage: The Story of Palestinian Struggle for Statehood* (Boston: Beacon, 2006)
The premier Palestinian political historian at Columbia University chronicles a twentieth-century history of Palestine and is critical of Palestinian failures.

Mearsheimer, John, and Walt, Stephen, *The Israel Lobby and U.S. Foreign Policy* (New York: Farrar, Straus & Giroux, 2007)
A controversial critique of US foreign policy by leading scholars at Harvard and Chicago. The book argues that US foreign policy in the Middle East is shaped less by American national interest than by the Israel lobby in Washington.

Morris, B., *1948: A History of the First Arab–Israeli War* (New Haven: Yale University Press, 2009)
An important and controversial study of Israel's early history by the leading Jewish historian at Ben Gurion University, Israel.

Nathan, S., *The Other Side of Israel: My Journey Across the Jewish/Arab Divide* (New York: Talese, 2005)
A British Jew with South African roots moves to Tel Aviv – then into an Arab village *within Israel* and is reminded of what she saw in South Africa. A vivid first-person narrative.

Netanyahu, Benjamin, *A Durable Peace: Israel and Its Place Among the Nations* (New York: Warner, 2000)
A conservative Israeli politician – now its prime minister – makes his case for Israel's future.

Pappe, Ilan, *The Ethnic Cleansing of Palestine* (Oxford: Oneworld, 2006)
An Israeli "post-Zionist" historian courageously reconstructs the controversial events of 1948 and demonstrates Israel's strategy for ethnic cleansing.

Rabinowitz, Dan, and Abu-Baker, Khawla, *Coffins on Our Shoulders: The Experience of Palestinian Citizens of Israel* (Berkeley: University of California Press, 2005)
A remarkable book by a Jewish and an Arab sociologist charting their different families' experience in Israel through multiple generations.

Raheb, Mitri, *I am a Palestinian Christian* (Minneapolis: Fortress, 1995)
A Palestinian Lutheran pastor in Bethlehem tells his story of growing up under occupation and his call to ministry. A first-hand account of the occupation of the West Bank from within.

Rees, Matt, *Cain's Field: Faith, Fratricide and Fear In the Middle East* (New York: Free Press, 2004)

Time magazine's Jerusalem bureau chief describes the internal divisions tearing apart both Arab and Israeli society. A user-friendly book for those just getting started.

Ross, Dennis, *The Missing Peace: The Inside Story of the Fight for Middle East Peace* (New York: Farrar, Straus & Giroux, 2004)

As special negotiator for both the Bush (Sr.) and Clinton administrations, Ross gives an "insider's story" of the Israel–Palestine conflict from 1988 to 2001.

Spencer, Carol, *Danger Pay: Memoir of a Photojournalist in the Middle East, 1984–1994* (Austin: University of Texas Press, 2008)

Spencer contends that how we frame photographs determines how "real life" is packaged for the Western consumer and that this has shaped Western understandings (misunderstandings?) of the Middle East.

Index of biblical and ancient sources

148